PRAISE FOR *ALMOST ROMANCE*

"When Howie met Nancy more than thirty years ago, they both had a lot to learn about love—and themselves. Nancy Balbirer's new memoir, *Almost Romance*, tells the story of two people (writer Balbirer and Howard J. Morris, cocreator of *Grace and Frankie*) who were always meant to be together if they could just get it together. And finally, in their fifties, they do. Fun and frothy and full of great callbacks to sex in the city over the last three decades, Almost Romance gives hope to romantics in an impersonal age for love. From Nancy's first anguished email reaching out to her old friend Howie, we are rooting for this couple, who come to realize that, after lives spent living without each other, they can't exist apart. Nora Ephron would approve."

—Nancy Jo Sales, author of
Nothing Personal: My Secret Life in the Dating App Inferno

"*Almost Romance* is a modern-day romantic thriller, because what could be scarier for a cynical New York divorcée than believing in love again? Balbirer's memoir spans the decades of missed opportunities with her soul mate from college. She is ballsy, insecure, and wickedly funny and overthinks everything. It's a great ride and a great read!"

—Josann McGibbon, Emmy-nominated screenwriter of
The Starter Wife and *Runaway Bride*

"The laugh-out-loud wit and astute contemporary observations that distinguish Nancy Balbirer's previous memoirs is on full display in this marvelous third book. She also gives us a deeply emotional, romantic story that makes us yearn for the two longtime friends to at last find happiness with each other."

—Charles Busch, actor, playwright, cabaret entertainer, novelist,
and screenwriter

Almost Romance

ALSO BY NANCY BALBIRER

Take Your Shirt Off and Cry
A Marriage in Dog Years

Almost Romance

A Memoir

Nancy Balbirer

Little

Published by Little A, New York

www.apub.com

Amazon, the Amazon logo, and Little A are trademarks of Amazon.com, Inc., or its
affiliates.

FINALE (from "Pippin")
Music and Lyrics by STEPHEN SCHWARTZ
© 1972 (Renewed) Stephen Schwartz
All Rights Administered by EMI BMPC CORP. (ASCAP) and
JOBETE MUSIC CO., INC.
All Rights for JOBETE MUSIC CO., INC. Controlled and Administered by
EMI APRIL MUSIC INC. (ASCAP)
3Print Rights for EMI BMPC CORP. Controlled and Administered by
ALFRED MUSIC.
All Rights Reserved.
Used by Permission of ALFRED MUSIC

ISBN-13: 9781542022828 (hardcover)
ISBN-10: 1542022827 (hardcover)

ISBN-13: 9781542022804 (paperback)
ISBN-10: 1542022800 (paperback)

Cover design by Holly Ovenden

All interior photos courtesy of the author

Printed in the United States of America

First edition

For Howie—then, now, always.

*And for any person who believes that love is a parade
that has passed them by, this book is for you too.*

AUTHOR'S NOTE

Some names and identifying characteristics have been changed in the interest of protecting privacy.

PRELUDE

From: Nancy Balbirer <REDACTED>
Date: August 28, 2014, at 4:39 PM
To: Howard <REDACTED>
Subject: Hi Howie

So. Where do I begin? Where did we leave off?

Yes, I dumped the big-shot director (aka "Darth Vader").

OMG, Howie—what a NIGHTMARE.

Total freak show.

I dunno what it was—loneliness, boredom, hunger for attention—not sure, but somehow I ended up dating this guy I wasn't even remotely attracted to when I first met him for FIVE MONTHS. In fairness, I *tried* to break up with him several times and then just either chickened out or got convinced to stay. But the second he started wanting to wear a dog collar and have me do him up the poop-shoot with a strap-on, I said, SORRY, HON, BUT THIS IS WHERE I STEP OFF THE BUS.

It's called "pegging," by the way—when a girl straps on a plastic penis and ventures forth into the anal playground. Isn't that interesting? How great is Google?

Now, look—I am no prude. But, at this point, sex tho' I do LOVE, I really am, I guess, what some people would call *vanilla* (which, by the way, IS A FLAVOR).

I don't do humiliation; I don't use "props" and I'm not into "role-play" (unless, of course, there's an Equity contract). Oh, OK—I will "role-play" but in a HOT way which does not include "scripts" wherein I am referred to as "Supreme Mistress" (!!!???!), or wherein I have to whip some poor schmuck with his own Brooks Brothers belt—NO.

Darth Vader took me everywhere and introduced me to EVERYONE; we went to all sorts of la-di-da events—screenings, parties, Broadway openings, and even some closings. So, imagine this: We go to the closing of the musical *The Bridges of Madison County*. You know the story, right? Lady has an unlikely affair with some hippie photographer and almost leaves her family because she is so desperately in love, blah, blah, blah. Well, if you thought the movie was a weepie, you should have gotten a load of the musical. It was beautiful and heartbreaking and deeply, deeply moving, made all the more so by the sad fact that the show got mixed reviews and couldn't find an audience of gays and women who wanted to see this shit. Anyway. I cried my eyes out, basking in the romance and love and sexed-up narrative of it all; I found it all terribly cathartic. Afterward, we go back to his house in Montauk and . . . ?

He wants me to tie him up with a dog leash, slap him, and tell him he doesn't deserve me.

It was like watching a double feature of *Love Story* and *Last Tango in Paris*.

I mean—I felt like Eva Braun with this guy!

So I told him, you know, NO; this is not my thing, I have said over and over, this is not my thing, but Darth Vader is, as we know, a director (and a very good one), so naturally he starts trying to convince me *I am this person*, telling me shit like I couldn't know I don't dig something I have never tried. The fuck kind of logic is this?? Just because I *haven't tried* something doesn't make it any *more* something I SHOULD try just by virtue of my not having tried it! But, as you know, I **was** always good at improvisation, so I figure *OK, maybe it's time to think outside my box.*

I *try* to do these things on his "menu" and . . . I just fall over laughing. I. Could. Not. Do. It.

So I break up with him; I go: "I'm very sorry but we are not compatible" and he goes:

"In what way, do you feel we are not compatible?"

For real.

So I go: "Well, for starters . . . *sexually*, but, you know, also I just don't feel like there is enough of a **spiritual connection** (yes, I went there). I do not feel there is a future, and if I am to introduce someone—a man— to my daughter, there has to be, that's my litmus test" (he had wanted to meet her). Darth Vader, of course, doesn't take **no** for an answer; **no** to this guy just means maybe he has to come up with a better way to wangle it into a **yes**. On and on and on and on—dude would **not** leave me alone, writing/ calling/texting me constantly, saying how he seriously thought we'd GET MARRIED at some point!!!!

OMG, Howie. Really.

The whole episode scared me off dating because, for a while there, before it got super freaky, I thought I might be falling for him. It scared me—*I* scared *myself*. How in God's name did I get involved with him, even to the point I did?? I mean, I'm not desperate (or I don't *feel* des- perate) and yes, I want male attention and to feel pretty and to have sex, but AT WHAT COST? I mean, whatever happened to taking a shower together? Or fucking on the floor or eating strawberries together?? Is all that too tame? Am I an old lady? You know what—I'm OK with that. One of my closest friends (who's also my neighbor), Nathaniel, was like: "As a gay man I feel like I've heard everything and STILL this story man- ages to horrify—HOWEVER, on the plus side—without even going full Rihanna—you *would* look really hot in a leather dominatrix getup!" and, OK, maybe I would, but that's not the point! (BTW—I'm actually OK with costumes, but no props!)

Meanwhile, after 4 years of being separated, my divorce is (God willing) almost final.

It looks like—fingers crossed—I'm about to sell my next book.

The Bear (yes, I still call her that) is 9½ and she is doing so well; she is a wonderful kid and I'm so lucky to be her mom.

I hope you are well—you SEEM well and how could you not be, working with Jane Fonda & Lily Tomlin? I can't wait to see it!

I love you and miss you, Howie. When am I gonna see you? We really, really should have an affair or a relationship. Isn't it about time, already? After 31 years? Seriously—do you have better chemistry with anyone else on the planet? Do I? I guess we were always destined (doomed?) to be just great friends, but I will never not believe we'd have made a great pair (sans strap-ons!!)!

Write me back and tell me everything . . .

Xoxoxoxoxo
Nancy

PART ONE

The Russian Samovar

April 24, 2015

Two things confused me as I sat in the front bar of the Russian Samovar on West Fifty-Second Street, ordering Dirty Martinis with a woman I didn't really know. One was that a beloved fictional character had once described the Samovar color scheme as being "very red" when, aside from the boudoir lights, it's actually sort of green, and the other was my reason for being in this more-green-than-red joint in the first place.

The woman sitting across from me that chilly spring Friday was a fancy Hollywood television producer named Candace Kahn. I say I didn't really know her because, aside from our having a three-second conversation twenty years before at a house party in Los Angeles, I really didn't. The week before our rendezvous, I had received a rather admiring direct Facebook message from **Candace Kahn**, a person I hadn't thought about in at least a decade, in which she gushed that she was a "fan" of my work and of me "in general." She mentioned that she was on the writing staff of my friend Howie's new TV show and this, plus the fact that she and I had "a gazillion people in common," meant that we "ABSOLUTELY MUST" get together for drinks when she was in New York the following weekend. She signed off with "I'll buy!" punctuated by a wink emoji.

At first I was like, *Wow, how cool is this,* because, after all, it's not every day you receive a flattering Facebook communiqué (usually I only get solicited for penis enlargements or for membership to Christian Mingle—Facebook knows me so well . . .). But almost immediately I went from delighted to baffled because this wasn't just flattering—it was flattering-with-a-soupçon-of-what-the-fuck. I read, then reread the message, hoping to glean more, but then ended up spending basically the entire morning muttering, "OK, lady, you like me—you really, REALLY like me, but . . . why, **exactly**, are you reaching out?" at my computer screen.

I wanted answers but was open to theories.

"Maybe she wants to option your book for television?" suggested my friend Jo, an actress who happened to be one of the aforementioned "gazillion people" Candace and I had in common. Jo had once performed in a musical Candace had co-written, but still, she knew Candace about as well as I did.

"Wasn't she a writer on *Friends*?" Jo asked.

"Yup," I said, "and *Sex and the City* . . ."

"So, maybe she wants to develop some sort of project with you?" she posited.

Maybe. But if that were the case, wouldn't she have just said so? Even if she didn't want to get into specifics, if it were about a project, wouldn't she have mentioned it or somehow woven it into the honeyed mix? Anyway, there was nothing to lose and only one way to find out, so I messaged back the enigmatic Candace Kahn and told her I was in.

I'm having dinner at 8 PM in the theatre district with a friend the Friday you're in town, I wrote, but could meet for a drink?

Perfect! she'd responded. I have theatre tickets that night—we could meet at 6:45—I love to go to the theatre tipsy!

Where should we meet? I asked her.

You pick! ☺ she volleyed back.

"Tell her you wanna meet at the Samovar," advised my friend Eddie, a high-end Manhattan tour guide for rich people or groups or groups of rich people.

"Why there?"

"Because this is all feeling very Russian novel-y to me—like something out of Pushkin or *The Master and Margarita* . . . Anyway, she's in television—she can afford the Samovar . . ."

And so it was that we settled on Russian Samovar, housed in what was once the fabled Sinatra haunt Jilly's Saloon, and a place neither of us had theretofore ever been.

When I arrived a few minutes before the appointed time, the Samovar scene, in full pre-theater swing, was packed, lively, and feeling no pain. I swanned about, keeping my eyes peeled, and just as I turned to head back toward the front, I saw her—a glamazon with aubergine-streaked hair and crimson lips—swing through the entrance. We locked eyes, and in a manner I can only describe as "seventies hair commercial," Candace Kahn and I, two sorta-strangers, slo-mo dove into each other's arms for an extravagant hug that for some reason felt neither weird nor inappropriate, after which we slid into chairs at a tiny table opposite the long wooden bar. In a flash, we found ourselves tucked into two *very dirty* and *very dry* Ketel One martinis and an overfamiliar confab about her son and my daughter and her troubled marriage and my divorce that, like our hug, felt both excessively chummy and inexplicably normal. Twenty minutes of maniacal oversharing and boozing went by, and just as my attention began to drift to the mysteries of the Samovar decor and why in the hell I was actually there, Candace suddenly shifted gears:

"OK," she said, "can I just cut to the chase?"

"Please—"

"I need to talk to you about Howard," she said slowly.

Howie? Why does she need to talk to me about Howie?

Perhaps it was the gravity in her tone—or maybe I was just caught off guard by the subject—but as soon as those eight words landed in my court, my vodka buzz, at the peak of its bloom, evaporated, and in its place a frantic tap-dance routine commenced in the center of my chest.

"Is he . . . OK?" I asked.

"He's fine," she said. "Well, actually, he's fine *now*—you heard about the embolism?"

"THE WHAT?"

"He had a pulmonary embolism—"

"WHEN?"

"A few months ago."

"Oh my god—is he OK?"

"He's fine."

"Oh my god—"

"I'm sorry to spring this on you."

"How did I not know this?"

"I think, I don't know—he was super depressed about it."

"Oh my god."

"And freaked out."

"Of *course*."

"But this also made him, I think, realize he needs to be living his life . . . differently."

"Health-wise, you mean?"

"Well, sorta, but more like he needs to be living his life more fully. Which is why I'm here tonight . . . why I . . . reached out to you."

Candace paused for a beat, then took my hands in hers.

"Howard's pretty crazy about you. And . . . you need to know that."

As stunned as I was by both this news and the way it was relayed *(this was why she'd cajoled me to meet with her?)*, I responded without missing a beat, as if some part of my being had anticipated this moment for a long time.

"Are you kidding me?" I practically shouted. "I've been in love with him for almost thirty-two years!"

Now it was Candace's turn to be stunned.

With hands still entwined on the table and the remnants of our cloudy cocktails between us, Candace and I sat for a few seconds, just staring at each other mutely. For two chicks who traffic in words, we were suddenly completely devoid of them.

"Well," she said finally, her eyes misting ever so slightly. "I think it's safe to say, the feeling is mutual."

~

Greenwich Village, 1983

I am a seventeen-year-old freshman drama major at NYU, walking into the Brittany Hall on East Tenth Street to see my friend Claire, with whom I grew up in a small Connecticut town. When I arrive, Claire is out, so I leave her a message with "the Desk Guy," a nineteen-year-old sophomore also-drama-major whose name is Howard, but whom everyone calls Howie.

Howie, the Desk Guy.

I happen to have a thing for Howie, the Desk Guy.

Everything about him turns me on: the sandy, middle-parted, feathered-back hair; the stubbly remnants of his Serpico beard; the giant John Hinckley aviator eyeglasses; the Boston accent; the fact that without permission or apology he reads (and comments on) every note I leave with him intended for someone else. My crush on him is such that every single time I see him behind the Brittany message desk and say, "Hi, Howie," it is by no means just a simple salutation; it is without question grade A flirting in the most brazen, unabashed way I have ever flirted with anyone in all my seventeen years. "Hi, Howie," I purr, leaning in toward him across the message desk. "Hey!" he says, grinning and leaning in toward me, as if our mutual instinct is to simply pour ourselves into each other. Over the next few years, I will visit Howie, the Desk Guy, as often as I can, inventing reasons to come to Brittany and leave messages just so I can "Hi, Howie" him into a squirming, blushing, heap of horny who will respond by flirting back just as shamelessly until there is nothing left to do (with our clothes on) but laugh.

~

How did it happen that the cosmos cracked open and out of its boundless sky descended Candace Kahn, in her pink Glinda bubble of goodness as an emissary between me and one of my oldest and dearest friends, the ship I'd always assumed had passed me in the night, but somehow in the middle of life in the middle of midtown, I was suddenly in the middle of hearing another story entirely?

"Howard Morris was on my radar for years," Candace began. "A mentor of mine and another woman I know—actually there were a bunch of people over the years who I was close to, who had worked with Howard, and they all spoke of him in a way that just stuck in my head . . ."

Because of this, over time, Candace found that she was always sort of on the lookout for Howie, though she didn't get to actually meet him until the year before our drinks date, when she was hired to be a writer on *Grace and Frankie*, the new television show he'd co-created. Hitting it off immediately, they bonded during the show's first season in a way that made them both feel as though they'd been engaged in a conversation that had been going on for years. I heard in detail about what a fabulous boss he was; how his belief in his writers allowed them to believe in themselves, especially when the inevitable elusive storyline could make wrangling a script seem all but impossible.

"I remember once," Candace said, "when it was my episode, we'd outlined it and then, I don't know, I guess I started thinking maybe it wasn't working and that maybe it would be better to just scrap the whole fucking thing and start over, but Howard in his gentle but firm way wouldn't let me off the hook. He was like, 'Candace, it's a good story and you can't blow off a good story just because it's challenging.' And, of course, he was right and I figured it out and it was all fine, but, you know what I mean, just the way he dealt with me, the way he deals with everyone in this totally non-douchey way is just so special and so not typical, you know?"

I did know. But it occurred to me, as she was talking, that in over three decades of knowing Howie, I really *didn't* know—at least not this side of him, from the perspective of someone with whom he had worked. That, though I had been friends with him longer than practically anyone else in my life, there were many ways I *didn't* know him at all—certainly not as a boss or a showrunner or a television producer in his natural habitat. More than anything else, hearing her say that, I felt so proud of him that he had not only made a name for himself in a notoriously difficult and fickle business but had done so with the love and respect of his colleagues.

And speaking of which, it turned out that, according to Candace, she wasn't the only Howie fan among the staff of *Grace and Frankie*. She continued her Howie commercial by relaying that the writers on their show cared for him with a fervor (and an intrusiveness) that she'd really never seen in her twentysomething years in the business. The collective consensus was that the only thing Howard Morris lacked when they met him was the right woman, a notion that Howie did nothing whatsoever to disabuse. In fact, if anything, he encouraged their myriad critiques of his love life (or lack thereof) wholeheartedly.

"And this is why," Candace continued, "one day, a few months ago, while we were on a break, he shared your email with us."

"My what?" I said, thinking I must have misheard her.

"We heard your email," she repeated.

I had no idea what she was talking about.

"My email?" I asked. "What email?"

"The one that you wrote to Howard," she said sheepishly. "It was read aloud in the room."

I racked my brain, trying to remember my last communications with Howie but . . . nothing—I was totally blank.

"What was it about?" I asked.

Candace paused.

"The 'pegger,'" she said, after a beat. "You know," she added, "strap-on dude?"

Oh. Christ.

Oh. My. Fucking. God.

Darth Vader. She's talking about Darth Vader.

And for the second time that evening, I was rendered speechless and was to remain that way, trying to contain my horror, while Candace recounted the tale of How an Email I Wrote about My Five-Month Affair with a Powerful Director and His Penchant for "Pegging" Was Heard by a Pack of Hollywood Comedy Writers.

"The writers' room had been split into two groups," Candace began. "The one Howard was leading was him and six women and a gay guy named Bobby who was legendary in the writers' room for his daily dramatic readings of Barbra Streisand's *My Passion for Design*. 'I just received the greatest email,' Howard told us. 'And I need Bobby to read it aloud.'

"And—oh my god—Nancy," Candace gasped as plates of pelmeni and beef Stroganoff bounced by behind her head. "Your email was absolutely *enthralling*: witty, sublime, feisty, sexy . . . No one spoke a fucking word—we were all spellbound."

"Thank you," I said, suddenly no longer feeling mortified that my confidential correspondence had been given a staged reading and instead wishing emails could be reviewed in the book section of the *New York Times*.

"Then," Candace continued, "Bobby (as you) says something like, 'Howie, we've been such great friends and for so long, don't you think, after all these years, we'd make a great pair?' and . . . It was a drop-the-mic moment. Everyone turned to Howard with mouths agape. I said, 'If you don't marry this woman, I will.' Then he told us a bit about his history with you—how you'd always been there, this shimmering thread that wound through the days of his life, a bestie with whom he could be real, but more than a *friend* in the sense that beneath the surface there was always . . . more. 'The truth is, I'm in love with her,' he told us. 'And I always have been. But (sigh) . . . she lives in New York, so . . . that's that.'"

Candace's eyes widened.

"Looks were exchanged," she continued. "We. Were. Having. None. Of. It. One of the women in the room said, 'Um, Howard? Have you heard of this new invention called *airplanes*? It's this contraption that can actually take you from Los Angeles to New York and back?' Anyway, blah, blah, blah—we moved on, got back to work, but honestly all anyone kept thinking about was *How is he not with her?*

"Anyway, later that day I was in his office and we talked about you some more. He told me that you had haunted him for years. 'She has existed on the periphery of every single relationship I've ever had,' he said."

"Seriously?" I choked. "For real?"

"Yes!" Candace said. "And I was like, 'Howard, how can you not pursue this? How?' And he goes, 'Eh, she lives in New York; I live in LA . . . She's got a kid; I've got a kid . . . Anyway . . . It's a good story, but . . .'"

Candace paused.

"And, you know what I said to him?"

She leaned in so we were practically nose to nose.

"I said, 'It *is* a good story, Howard. And you can't blow off a good story just because it's challenging.'"

As much as you have to give ALL the slow claps to Candace for using her boss's very own words against him, the course of true love, as Shakespeare once said, never did run smooth, and as much as I adored this story—what with all the declarations of love and armies of overly invested, cheerleading buttinskies—it turned out to not be quite the *whole* story.

"We all hate his girlfriend," Candace announced.

"He has a girlfriend?"

"Yes, but she's terrible—"

"Yes, but . . . *he has a girlfriend?*"

"Yes. Well, you know something, no—that's not fair. He's in what I like to call . . . *a situation.*"

"Uh-huh, and what does *he* like to call it?"

"Look: he's sorta seeing this woman who he was seeing before for a while—"

"Ohhhh—you mean the blonde?"

"Yes, and he was going out with her—"

"I thought he broke up with her—"

"He did."

"OK . . ."

"But somehow, I don't know, it didn't . . . *take.* And he started seeing her again after not seeing her, and we were all like, 'Howard, you can't . . .'"

"But he is—"

"Yes, but no one understands why—including Howard."

"Maybe he loves her—"

"No, he definitely doesn't. NO. But he . . . Look," she continued, "she's terrible and *she's not even nice to him*, but I guess I don't know—haven't you ever gone out with someone against your better judgment, someone you weren't even really all that attracted to but somehow you got into it, and for whatever reason—not wanting to be alone, laziness, whatever, you just sort of stayed?"

"Given that some of my more humiliating emails are now being performed as minor theatricals, I think we both know the answer to that."

"You know how he is," Candace said, shaking her head. "I think he has trouble being alone . . ."

Candace was right—I *did* know how he was, which is why I suppose, even though I was incredulous about the girlfriend, I wasn't *that* incredulous because from the time I had known him, Howard Morris had always had a girlfriend (or a wife who, at one time, had been his girlfriend). First there was Sunny from Chicago, who was adorable and with whom he broke up in order to go out with Lois, whom he dated for six months before realizing that Lois had no idea they were going out—in her mind, they were just friends and never an item, which sent Howie not only reeling but back to Sunny, who by then had zero interest because, as I said, she was adorable and had moved on to someone else. Then there was Talia, the Canadian RA, whom Howie dated for several years until one day, a few years after they'd graduated from NYU, she went to the Kripalu Center for Yoga & Health in western Massachusetts and not only gave up her sexuality to the Sun God but gave up Howie too. Somehow, during all that time at NYU, no matter how much I dug Howie or how much he seemingly dug me, I was never his girlfriend.

And believe me—I tried.

~

Greenwich Village, 1984–85

My roommate Therese and I are having lattes at Caffe Reggio on MacDougal Street when Howie, the Desk Guy, and his girlfriend, Sunny, who also happen to be there, come by our table to say hello on their way out. After a brief conversation about nothing in particular, Howie and Sunny go on their merry way.

"Stop cockteasing Howie," Therese admonishes. "He belongs to Sunny."

"I wasn't cockteasing him—I barely said a word!"

"No," Therese says, eyeing me dubiously, "but you were thinking about it."

"How do **you** know what I was thinking?"

"Cuz I know—"

"OK, Uri Geller . . ."

"You're a cocktease and everyone knows it."

This is not exactly NOT true. I **am** a cocktease and a rather unabashed one at that. At barely eighteen, having fled the *Ice Storm*–y Connecticut hometown where I was bullied into believing I was a homely "play-gay" freak by my obnoxious-straight-out-of-*The-Official-Preppy-Handbook* classmates, I have now, for several splendiferous months, been enjoying the attentions of the many males—gay, straight, bi, and otherwise—littering and glittering our Washington Square campus. Making up for lost time and small tits, I am reveling in the Male Gaze; I have no objections to being objectified; I have a diaphragm and a cheerful attitude; I am footloose; I am fancy-free! I don't look too-too hard at my questionable choices or low standards—I am too busy looking for love and validation in all the wrong faces; too busy having "sex on my own terms," even though I haven't a clue what those terms **are** or what they will ultimately cost. I have taken to my new status like a kid in a candy store with a million dollars and a mouth full of sweet teeth ready, willing, and able to suck every confection that crosses my path to a fare-thee-well. I wear my "slut" badge with pride, not prejudice, and I wish Therese would cut me some slack, but of course she won't because not only is Sunny, aside from me, her best friend, BUT **what I don't know** in this moment is that Therese is a lesbian, and not only do **I** not know that Therese is a lez, but **Therese** doesn't know that Therese is a lez, and she won't know it until the following year when she will get very drunk at Panchito's Mexican Restaurant, come back to our dorm room, slip into my twin bed with me while I'm asleep and start fondling my tits. She will initially **vehemently** insist that the tit-fondling is because she had too many tequila shots and black-bean nachos with extra jack cheese and that made her temporarily forget she was straight, which might very well have seemed like a plausible explanation except that a few months before, when we went to her parents' empty rental apartment in the Bronx, she cajoled me into making out with her on the beige wall-to-wall shag carpeting for the entire duration of Spandau Ballet's "True," which was fine, but when I remind her of this incident and suggest that when you couple **that** with this latest, it **does** beg the "Are you perhaps-maybe gay" question, she gets so upset with me, she not only leaves the room, she also leaves school. Years later, when she finally embraces her sexuality (but still hates me), she will (unbeknownst to me) write an unflattering character based on me (a sort of Stepford-y zombie-princess who longs for bigger boobs) in a surrealist fantasia that will be performed as part of a "womyn's playwriting festival" at Dixon Place on the Lower East Side. Humiliated though I will be sitting there, wedged amid a junta of RadFems, clutching a bouquet of pink roses for my old roomie's very first produced writing effort, I will nevertheless be genuinely happy for Therese that she has found her calling—sapphic, scribal, whatever—and, putting my best Vanessa Redgrave-in-*Julia*-martyr-chic face on, I will hold my head high throughout the wretched proceedings.

But back to the cocktease at hand:

While, YES, it is true that my style these days is basically to fuck first, ask questions later, it is ALSO true that Howie is not exactly a choirboy (or whatever the Jewish equivalent is) and somehow, no matter where he is, relationship-wise, with all his girlfriends, real or imaginary, Howie has a way of finding me.

Like, EVERYWHERE.

I'm at Steve's Ice Cream on Sixth when someone behind me says, "Steve's is wicked ahhh-some—lawtsa tawpings . . ." in **that** accent, and when I turn, who's smiling back at me sheepishly?

OR I'm bartending the weekly Drama Department "Disorientation Party" (which somehow I've managed to finagle as my "crew requirement") when who do I see staring at me from across the room while I make, like, four million Dirty Russians for dissolute coeds who do not, at least outwardly, appreciate libations of such peerless sophistication?

OR I'm at my first day of a Drama Department–required class called Dreams and Dream Psychology, the purpose of which none of us quite ever understand beyond the fact that it's an easy A and WHO'S sitting right behind me?

In fact, it is because of this class that my acquaintance with Howie moves past awkward-but-exhilaratingly-flirtatious moments into true friendship. With time to kill after class, twice a week for a semester, Howie and I walk in circles around Washington Square Park, our conversation a tangle of tangents about theater, movies, music, food, our pre-NYU lives.

"Were you the star of your high school drama department too?" he asks one day.

"Wasn't everybody here?" I laugh. "We did mostly musicals, though . . ."

"Which ones?" he asks. "Who'd you play?"

"Dolly in *Hello, Dolly!*; Lola in *Damn Yankees* . . ."

"You seem like a Lola." He grins before adding, "Not that I don't like Nancy!"

"Fuckin' old-lady name . . ."

"Try bein' a Howard!"

"Howard's actually kinda cool."

"Yes, if you're a hundred and two!"

"Aw, come on—"

"I mean, I guess it's better than Murray!"

"**Definitely** better than Murray, my god . . ."

"How does a Murray get laid?"

"He doesn't—"

"Can you imagine having sex with someone named Murray?"

"No!" I say, cracking up so hard, I almost fall over.

"So, what you're telling me," Howie says, laughing at my laughing, "is that Murray's not fuckable?"

"Yes. I mean NO! Murray's not fuckable—"

"Poor Murray—"

"But Howard is . . ."

And with this, suddenly, for what feels like several minutes but is in reality about five seconds, laughing stops, looking at each other stops; we just keep moving, keep walking, eyes straight ahead, brains scrambling for words. AWKWARD! Finally, Howie gets us back to before the tangent.

"I got leads in the regular plays," he says, "but never got any good parts in the school musicals, and I can sing the fuck outta *Pippin*—"

"OH MY GOD YOU GUYS DID *PIPPIN*?"

"Yup."

Pippin, the darkly comic fairy tale about a young prince on a quest for passion, meaning, and his place in the world, is not just a cult classic but such a personal obsession of mine that in my freshman year I participated in an ill-advised workshop wherein we tried to adapt the 1,200-page novel *War and Peace* for the stage *only because* John Rubinstein, Broadway's original Pippin, was our fearless leader. While everyone else was rightfully concerning themselves with tsars and dowagers and French invasions, all I cared about was hearing John dish about what it was like to work with Bob Fosse. As soon as I tell Howie that not only do I LOVE *Pippin* but that it's one of my all-time favorites, we pause in front of the fountain and he begins singing Pippin's solo from the finale:

21

I'm not a river or a giant bird
That soars to the sea
And if I'm never tied to anything
I'll never be free . . .

"Holy shit, Howie!" I cry, totally blown away by his dulcet tenor. "HOW did they NOT cast you as Pippin?"

"Fuck if I know." He shrugs. "They cast some other putz . . . ," he says, before continuing to sing:

I wanted magic shows and miracles
Mirages to touch
I wanted such a little thing from life
I wanted so much

Skateboarders, students, and pot dealers continue to snake past us as I join him for the finale of the finale:

I never came close, my love
We nearly came near
It never was there
I think it was here . . .

Maybe it's because the ninety minutes prior have been spent discussing dreams—their interpretations, their significance, in life and in art—that these tête-à-têtes have about them the same sort of ethereal reverberation that continues to glow long after you're awake. It is also during one of these intense mega-convos that I first learn about Howie's Crohn's disease—the chronic intestinal malady that had resulted in numerous surgeries and wreaked havoc on his life—and the fact that once a week, after his desk shift, he saw a shrink. This to me was totally mind-blowing—I'd never met anyone that young who'd been to a shrink before.

"Is it fun?" I ask him.

"It's huge—"

"What's it like?"

"You'd love it—"

"Yeah?"

"You're perfect for it."

"Thank you!"

"No problem."

I can't know in this moment the extent to which Howie's assessments—pithy, poetic, and as spot-on as Obi-Wan Kenobi—will resonate in the years to come, but just like the time he said, "You have a great ass," his telling me that I am perfect for therapy causes my entire inner being to assume the kaleidoscopic flutter of a Busby Berkeley musical.

∿

"Anyway," Candace continued, "'girlfriend' is frankly a misnomer . . ."

"Friend with benefits?" I offered.

"Yeah, but without the *friend* or the *benefits* parts—her interest in him seems to boil down to can he get her tickets to see Ed Sheeran or not . . ."

Not that Howie knew Ed Sheeran—he didn't—just as he didn't know Larry David or Mick Jagger or the guy from *Daredevil*. But, according to Candace, the Not-Girlfriend, evidently keen to meet luminaries, was banking on the fact that Howie either knew *people* who knew those people or knew *people* who knew those people's *people*. After all, they lived in LA and though celebrity obsession is nothing new and certainly not a phenomenon unique to any particular place, one could argue that Los Angeles is its apogee. Perhaps owing in part to the relative proximity mere mortals have to gods and goddesses of the small or silver screen (in LA, if you walk out of a dressing room in a way-too-expensive boutique garbed in a way-too-expensive getup and someone who looks very much like Ringo Starr says, "You look *gawjus,*" and someone who looks very much like Barbara Bach agrees with him, it is definitely Ringo Starr and Barbara Bach (yes, that happened; yes, I bought it; yes, I was in debt for two years . . .), it's easy to see how in a town like that, one can get seduced into a concordant "we are one" headspace.

Of course, there's a difference between benign fascination and the more acute *idée fixe.* Listening to Candace describe the Not-Girlfriend's antics, I was reminded of how, during the years I lived in LA, I was never certain if it was desperation or pragmatism or some shaken-not-stirred cocktail of both that begot the "kinda-sorta-ness" to which a certain breed of the Hollywood-adjacent clung. To this genre of fame fanatic, it doesn't matter if they're six or six hundred degrees of separation from Kevin Bacon. Maybe their lot as a Viagra rep by day is a bit of a snooze, but if by night they can go to a party Leonardo DiCaprio is supposedly attending, they can believe their life is as stimulating as that of the dolls they're hawking. So they never even lay eyes on "Luscious Leo" and the most famous person they meet at the party is someone who introduces himself as John Wayne's grandson? The point is: *they're there.*

And speaking of there—even if everyone on the planet wanted me to believe the woman Howie was dating(ish) was a nonissue, **she** was **there** and, as I said to Candace, even "barely a thing" was still a thing, at least a thing to me.

"I hear you," Candace said, and we sat for a few seconds, deflated and subdued, staring into our now-vacant-save-for-the-toothpicks stemware.

"I have an idea!" Candace said, suddenly brightening. "I've written a play, and it's being produced by the Oregon Shakespeare Festival up in Ashland. A bunch of the writers—including Howard—are coming up to see it one weekend in June as sort of a writers' room field trip. What if *I* invited *you* and you just sort of *happened to show up* to that very same performance?"

My first thought (after *Where the fuck is Jaye P. Morgan with the gong?*) was that I really had to hand it to Candace. Because even if this cockamamie scheme seemed more like a rejected *Friends* episode than a viable plan ("The One Where Nancy Travels Three Thousand Miles to the Middle of Nowhere to Be Humiliated by a Man When She Could Have Just as Easily Achieved That on the C Train"), I couldn't help but be charmed by the quick-witted, prepossessing manner with which such *mishegoss* was proposed.

It was easy to imagine Candace in her wonted domain: perched in the various writers' rooms she'd been in for the last three decades, pitching storylines—some of them brilliant, some of them loopy, but all delivered with the same spark of unfettered glee. What was *not* so easy to imagine—at least not at the time—was that the same winning ebullience that contributed to Candace's success as a writer had made her an utter disaster in her side hustle as a matchmaker: She'd either set up people who despised each other upon sight or NOT set up people so well suited that when they'd fallen in love and found out they were each independently pals with (but not set up by) Candace Kahn, they'd be so furious with her for the oversight, she'd be expunged from their lives ever after. Only one couple, taking pity, invited Candace to the wedding she had no part whatsoever in instigating, but to get her back they seated her next to Jeremy Piven, who, though not yet famous, was already an unmitigated asshole.

After a staggering number of imbroglios, even Candace herself had to admit that, yenta-wise, she was one of the world's worst. So, publicly, she called it quits; privately, however, to assuage her unremitting yen, she furtively wrote the names of people she thought belonged together (or hoped would fall in love) on cocktail napkins, which she'd date and put into a drawer, hoping beyond hope that one day she'd be able to present one of her couples with a special memento. However, after years of napkins, the drawer was stuffed to the gills but with people who either didn't notice or didn't like each other (one was even filing a sexual harassment lawsuit against the one Candace had intended for her!), and eventually, having lost all faith in herself, Candace tossed the napkins and turned the drawer into a place to house her massive collection of staplers. And that was it—she vowed to never write on a napkin again.

Sitting there with her that night at the Samovar, having not the vaguest sense that the esteemed, terribly chic human sitting before me had the sort of checkered past that caused her husband to ban her from ever again meddling in the love lives of others, I thanked her for the bad *Friends* storyline suggestion before gently demurring.

"Honestly," I told her, "I think I'm a little too old and too tired for a stunt like that."

"I know, I know," Candace sighed. "I figured it was a stretch. But after hearing your email to him and then him telling us over and over: 'She's the one that got away,' I guess I thought—well, *we all* thought, really—as writers, we just wanted to see if we could fix the story. I mean, you're a writer—you get it . . ."

Oh, I got it all right. The impulse to rewrite, to *zhuzh*. But this "the one that got away" narrative was more than a tad problematic. I had heard it before vis-à-vis Howie and his feelings for me, and each time those five words were lobbed in my direction, a warm flutter of love and whatever I'd had for lunch would billow across the landscape of my innards. But the intoxication of being so described by someone I so admired would soon lap-dissolve into chagrin. Maybe it's me, but doesn't wistfully referring to someone as "the one that got away" suggest that this person "got away" completely of their own accord, slipping out through an unattended portal? But what if "the one" "got away" because, in fact, they were shoved out the door, bum's-rush style?

That's the story I remember.

~

1986

"I wrote a play," Howie is telling me. "You gotta read it—you're perfect to play this girl. Trust me."

Honestly, I've been hearing this kinda thing a lot lately. From the moment we were allowed to audition for stuff at school, I have been cast in every single role I've wanted to play, be it mainstage productions, studio productions, student productions, student films, student TV shows, whatever, and it's been a gas and a half—how could it not be? I'm busy, I'm OBSESSED, I devour plays like I do fun-size Snickers, and for the first time in my life, I'm like that Billy Squier song:

You never get awayyyyy . . . EVERYBODY WANTS YOU.

So what if the plays I'm doing at school are weird—my attitude is FUCK YEAH: the weirder, the more avant-garde, the more bizarre, THE BETTER. For the first major role I landed in my first full-scale NYU production, I played a fat, middle-aged, racist landlady from the Bronx in a surrealistic dream-play about race and how, in particular, it applied to women of color. Since in real life I am a slight, tomboyish brunette who looks maybe fifteen, I was costumed in the ugliest blonde wig you've ever seen, white Kabuki-style makeup, and a fat suit designed by the Tony Award–winning costume designer Willa Kim (which took sixteen hours of fittings!), and no one had a fucking clue it was me in there (talk about disappearing inside my role)! Now, like I said, the play dealt with race, but it's this trippy, nonlinear one-act centered around a biracial chick and the various characters (Queen Victoria, African nationalist Patrice Lumumba, Jesus Christ, etc.) who represent her nervous breakdown. I thought it was brilliant. Did I give a shit that basically everyone who came to see me in this thing was like, *What the fuck **is** this play?*

Nope.

I was completely psyched and loved every wacked-out minute of it.

After that, I was cast to play one of the artist Edward Gorey's illustrations come to life in a wild little revue of fables, music, and dance called *Tinned Lettuce*, which was about . . .

Actually, I don't really know what it was about.

Quite frankly, no one did. Once, when I asked Edward Gorey (a very nice man who was into cats and raccoon coats and classic Keds sneakers) what "tinned lettuce" meant and what it was about, he just looked at me and laughed and laughed and laughed. When I asked our director, Daniel Levins (a guy who'd been a principal dancer at American Ballet Theatre and also played the bitchy choreographer in the movie *The Turning Point*), what it was about, I was told: "To over-interpret or inject meaning into an artist's work or motives—even with the most innocently constructive intentions—is more often than not a search for self-importance," which was kind of a long way of saying, "I don't know what the fuck it's about; please, get over yourself."

When the *New York Times* came to see it, they at least called it "merrily macabre," but I don't think they knew what it was about either.

Be that as it may, this cool-as-shit-theatrical-whatever-the-fuck, which was being co-produced by NYU and this rich guy who was dating Laurie Anderson, became a massive cult hit that got extended and extended, and suddenly there was interest in an off-Broadway transfer, so we had this backer's audition where we performed select scenes and dances and sang our guts out at a rehearsal studio on Lafayette Street while the big-time producer Manny Azenberg slept in the front row on a foldout chair. He must have been pretty tired cuz it was the middle of the day and we were LOUD. For a show no one understood or could even begin to describe, a whole lot of exciting stuff went down: channel 5 News came by to . . . I don't know . . . I guess try to figure out what the hell we were up to, and why everyone was losing their shit over this show, and in the course of interviewing Edward for the segment, they decided to also feature ME, performing my role as a neglected and abused child named Theodora, who, rescued by a troupe of theatrical bats, ends up the toast of vaudeville. It was only the local news, but still, lots of people saw it including my manic-depressive cousin on Long Island who was so starstruck (and mid–manic episode) that she stayed up all night baking hundreds of chocolate-chip cookies for the whole cast, then hand-delivered them to our shared dressing room the next day.

But the most **awesome** thing that happened during the run of *Tinned Lettuce* (aside from the time we all had dinner with Laurie Anderson at Indochine) was during a curtain call, as I was taking my bow, I heard someone screaming, **"Brava! Brava! Braaaavaaaaa!"** only to discover that it was none other than Mikhail Fucking Baryshnikov.

Uh-huh.

Fucking, by the way, is his middle name. It's Russian for "COULD ANYONE BE HOTTER THAN ME?"

Afterward, "Misha" came sweeping backstage to hug me (YES) and as I stood there, nose to nose (he's five five) with the face that was every-girl-in-America's bedroom poster, he goes:

"Your eyes make me cry, but your hands make me laugh!"

And just like I had no fucking clue what "tinned lettuce" meant, I didn't know what the hell Misha meant either, but he was SUCH a fox it was like, *Who cares what he means?* **Who cares what any of it means?** I'm not interested in making waves (unless it's a play about waves that no one understands); I'm interested in MAKING ART. I'm a "karma, karma, karma, karma, karma chameleon" on a quest for **importance**, not, as my director admonished, **self-importance**! I am about THE WORK, THE ART OF BEHAVING PRIVATE IN PUBLIC and becoming the next Eleonora Duse. And so far, it's going pretty great! My peers are digging me, seeing my work and asking me to consider their projects, like this past fall when I was asked to play the vixenish boss-lady Madame in a production of *The Maids*, Jean Genet's psychodrama about class warfare, sadomasochism, and bad help. With the exception of one tiny-but-crucial scene toward the end, I spent almost the entirety of the action offstage while the titular maids—engaged in a full-on folie à deux—obsess about my character, fantasizing ways to murder me. That our British student director was more interested in partying at Area or Palladium or Danceteria than attending rehearsals made no nevermind to me; I worked on my role with my new teacher, David Mamet, into whose highly selective scene-study class I had just been invited, on how to make my performance "director-proof." Mamet, whose teaching style is basically tart-tongued Talmudic scholar meets the Great Santini, instructed me that whether the director's off doing blow with the rest of the club kids or he's just a dumb-fuck with his head up his ass, **my** performance is **my** responsibility and must kill regardless. The callow grandiosity with which I milked my cameo after working with my high-flown teacher made me believe that even if I was offstage, the specter of my character's presence would hover over the proceedings, like Gene Tierney in *Laura*, whose absence only served to make her seem all the more present. None of this, however, made our little pageant work—not my attempts at evoking Gene Tierney; not my FABULOUS Edwardian-era aubergine gown; not my Evelyn Nesbit "Gibson Girl" hairdo; and certainly not the two chicks playing the maids, both of whom had unfortunately failed to "director-proof" their performances. This thing wasn't just surreal or nonlinear—it was a flop! And what's worse, the space in which we played our thankfully short run was so small, it made the cheerless faces of the audience—which, night after night, fled even before the curtain call was over—completely visible. Most of the time I did my best to ignore their miserable mugs, yet the evening Howie attended I couldn't help but fixate on him, sitting in the second row, clutching his rolled-up program and looking bewildered. I felt torn about him seeing me in this fiasco, but as embarrassing as it was, and no matter how much I was like, *Oh my god, please don't let him think I'm lame for being in this mess,* he was there because of course he was. Whether it's great, whether it's crap, whether there's weather, steadfast, loyal Howie didn't miss a single thing I was in. *Oh my god, I love him,* I thought as I swanned about the stage, knocking back fake champagne, as my character becomes more and more aroused, fantasizing a life of crime, *I LOVE HIM!*

"You should be doing comedy," he told me afterward as I stood in the pathetic aftermath, still in my FABULOUS costume, and he in his ginormous parka, while crew members and stragglers milled about. "You're funny," he said.

Funny? I internally fumed. *Comedy?* Does he **not** understand that I AM A **SERIOUS** ACTRESS WHO WILL HAVE A **SERIOUS** CAREER IN WHICH I ROUTINELY BREAK PEOPLE'S HEARTS WITH MY SHATTERING PERFORMANCES IN ALL MANNER OF **SERIOUS** ACTRESS ROLES?!

Perturbed though I was by his assessment, I could never be too-too mad at him because I am too-too mad **about** him. I am a junior now and he is a senior. It has been two years since I first handed him a note behind the Brittany message desk and by now he is one of my most cherished friends. We see each other's performances; we prize each other's feedback and encouragement. Our conversations continue to be funny, fiery meditations on anything and everything—a dialogue perpetually in progress, with no beginning and no end, only a giddy middle that is so intoxicating, so gratifying, I almost forget how bad I want to fuck him.

Almost.

Anyway, I thanked him for coming and we hugged for the first time ever, a hug that, I must say, lasted an awfully long time for a guy supposedly in a "serious" relationship with Talia, the Canadian RA. We stood wrapped around each other, first completely frozen, then awkwardly shifting weight from one foot to the other, as if we were sixth graders gamely braving their first "Stairway to Heaven."

"I dig your parka," I said, not because I really cared for it or about it, but because it seemed like a less pervy declaration than "I dig how your jeans are ever so slightly faded at the crotch."

"It's . . . uh . . . an 'irregular' from, uh . . . Marshalls," Howie mumbled into my Evelyn Nesbit "Gibson Girl" hairdo. "But, you know, very warm . . ."

Pleeeease don't let this feeling end; it's everything I am, everything I want to be, I thought to myself, my lust not only off the charts but apparently cribbing lyrics from the "Theme from *Ice Castles*."

"The irregularity does not diminish the, uh, warmth," Howie continued.

"Uh-huh."

"Like, at all."

"I can feel . . ."

"Feel what?"

"The warmth—"

"It can actually get too hot sometimes."

"I bet," I said, sliding my arms inside his sleeves so that we were chest to chest.

"I HAVE A DISEASE," Howie said, suddenly pulling back and holding me at arm's length.

"You mean the Crohn's?" I asked.

"Yes—"

"So?"

"And a girlfriend—"

"Well," I said, "Crohn's seems manageable, but I hear girlfriends can kill you . . ."

Howie laughed and then so did I, and then we stood there laughing until the laughter died down and we were suspended in that weird space of nothing to say and everything to say, just sorta staring at each other. Finally, Howie came to enough to pierce the weirdness.

"Comedy," he said, shaking his rolled-up program at me. "That's your thing. Trust me."

"*Trust me,*" he had said then.

"Trust me," he is saying now, "you are perfect to play this girl in my play."

I had vowed, after my experience with *The Maids*, to never again participate in a student production; I will stick with the mainstage productions directed by honest-to-god theater professionals, who, even if they can't always tell me what it's about, at least, I told myself, know what they are doing. But almost immediately after making this promise to myself, I will break it. "I wrote a play. You gotta read it . . ."

And on a rainy afternoon over Christmas break, as I sit in a rental car in the parking lot of a Winn-Dixie supermarket in Key Largo, Florida, I begin to read the pages that by the time I finish I know signify the beginning of the rest of his life. I laugh, I cry, just like those tourists in those dumb commercials when they're interviewed outside Broadway shows, because I know, I just know.

He has done it.

Howie has been writing plays for pretty much the whole time he's been an acting student and he's put on quite a few, and they were good. But this? This is different. This is on a whole nother level. And suddenly, I can't think of anything else but this play called *Almost Romance*. Howie's play. Howie's fucking beautiful, amazing, hysterically funny, heartbreaking play about a boy who loves a girl who doesn't love him back even though he believes that, in her heart of hearts, she really does. The play takes the audience—occasionally addressing them directly—through the relationship the girl maintains is strictly one of "just friends," and concludes with the boy seeing that, in the end, the girl was right. Or at least accepting that this is the true way she felt. "Maybe she wasn't the girl *of* my dreams," the boy tells the audience in the denouement, "she was the girl *in* my dreams, a girl I dreamed about . . ."

I need to do this play.

I need to do this part.

I'm not quite sure, at this point, how to play a contemporary young woman, someone not unlike myself, conflicted about love and relationships and how best to navigate them while at the same time being a paragon of feminism. It would be, in many ways, my scariest, most challenging role yet: What would I do without the facade of the fat suit, without the cloak of the cartoon character, without the smoke-screened self?

But for now, if the **thought** of playing Howie's heroine terrifies me, the actual process of playing her will thrill me: for almost the entire spring semester, from late January when the official casting is announced until late April, I will be spending pretty much every single day with the person I have spent over two years wanting to spend every single day with.

"I hope you're OK with making out with Howard Morris," Howie had said to me when he first handed me the script. "Cuz he'll be the guy playing opposite you."

I am more than OK with this. (I am decidedly less OK about having to **also** make out with **the other** actor in our cast, an arrogant, misogynistic jackass who will one day become very famous for, among other things, being an arrogant, misogynistic jackass.)

Now, some chicks might care that their first kiss with a guy about whom they're cuckoo for Cocoa Puffs takes place not after dinner and a movie but instead under imaginary circumstances in front of several note-taking onlookers, but I am not that chick! I am the chick who, when she gets to deliver her first lines—"I want you. I want you more than I've ever wanted anything. Kiss me. Kiss me passionately."—DOESN'T HAVE TO DO ANY ACTING AT ALL! And I have to believe Howie feels the same way, because from our very first rehearsal, from the second our stage manager, Sue "Q" Hoffmann, reads the opening stage direction, "He goes to her and gives her the most passionate

If it strikes me that "legal time" is a meaningless phrase devised by a dude with a girlfriend who wants to have his cake and fuck it too, it certainly doesn't stop me. Why would it? The on-again, off-again thing I have with the "Young Republican" film major who's good-in-bed-but-treats-me-like-shit is yet again in off-again mode, and the guilt I feel toward Howie's Canadian RA is assuaged by my inherent belief that, relationship-wise, college, or more specifically "art school," is a wild and woolly four-year free-for-all, governed by an imprecise and ephemeral code of ethics with more partner swapping than a square dance. Maybe in the sanctity of the suburban homes our teachers implore us to never visit again, lest our progress with them be ruined, we'd be scandalized by the mere thought of something as skanky and unsavory as head lice, but here at NYU, when an entire cast of *Hamlet* gives each other crabs, no one bats a fucking eye. All bets (and most tops) are off and being "cool" about "whatever" is where it's at, at least until the day comes when someone's "cool" begins to evaporate and in its place arrives a mass of complicated feelings. That day will come for me, but not yet. Because before we get to the dalliance Howie and I enact in order to delight our hormones is the one we enact in order to delight our audiences. And delight them we do: For the five shows we perform over the course of our three-day run, it is standing room only, with explosive laughter and deafening applause. *Almost Romance* is a smash beyond anything we could have hoped; everyone who comes to see us loves it, including a director friend of mine who is so smitten, she decides she'd like to remount it as part of a one-act comedy festival at a renowned off-Broadway theater company. Off-Broadway?! This would mean my first professional job and I'm only a junior!

"You'll have to read for it," my director-friend tells me, "but it's just a formality for the producer," she coos. There will come a time when I will replay this moment in my mind, searching every frame as if it's the Zapruder film, for any clue of equivocation or foreboding, but now I only feel as if what we have built together, Howie and I, has taken on a life of its own. All we need to do is sit back and enjoy the ride.

If only I had remembered to wear a seat belt.

"You guys are so in love," my friend Paola gushes a few weeks after the show has closed when I run into her on the street. "It's so beautiful."

"He doesn't love me, though," I tell her sadly.

"Of course he does!" she practically shouts. "Oh my god—it's soooo obvious and everybody knows it."

"He's seeing someone else," I counter. "He has a girlfriend."

Paola smiles. "Yeah, yeah, yeah—maybe he won't admit it. *Yet.*" She laughs. "But believe me—he does."

Paola gives me a big hug before rushing east on Tenth Street, and once she's gone, I burst into tears and cry all the way back to my dorm.

What I am too embarrassed to tell Paola is that I'd had a conversation with Howie one day over brunch at Elephant & Castle in which I asked him pointedly WHY I couldn't be his girlfriend. We had gone there, to our favorite spot, for our favorite cheeseburgers, to have a postmortem in the wake of our theatrical triumph. Playing the object of Howie's character's affection, the months and months of rehearsal and making out and his leaving me flirty notes, all of it, every day, had made me believe that though a relationship wasn't in the cards for our alter egos, the happy ending to our real-life romance was all but a fait accompli. The problem was that there was another person whose amorous feelings had been stirred by our passionate portrayal and that would be Talia, the Canadian RA. Busy with her own affairs (work, love, what-have-you), Talia had been so off our radar and so out of the picture, I, at least, had all but forgotten about her. Then, after saying she was so busy it was unlikely she'd be able to even see the show at all, she turned up, ringside, opening night. Waning interest or not, watching her boyfriend make out with another chick apparently had such an aphrodisiacal effect that Talia's long-dormant ardor was reawakened and suddenly the only "busy" Talia was getting was with Howie. When I learned of this felicitous rekindling and my unwitting aiding and abetting, I was dumbfounded: How, I wanted to know, were we not running off into the sunset together? Our chemistry was undeniable. I knew that what I was feeling was real; I knew I wasn't alone in feeling it. What ensued was a litany of reasons why, according to Howie, I couldn't be his girlfriend.

"You're not Jewish enough," he said for openers. "And you smoke . . ."

"OK."

"Guys are constantly checking you out, which doesn't seem to bother you cuz you're MASSIVELY insecure," he continued.

"True," I conceded.

"And TOTALLY neurotic—"

"Also true."

"I mean—I've NEVER met anyone more neurotic!"

"I'm sorry—have you met YOU?"

"YOU WEAR BLACK ALL THE TIME!"

"So?"

"I JUST DON'T HAVE TIME FOR THAT KIND OF AGGRAVATION!" he shouted.

Well.

For once, I was speechless. How was it possible, after our tour de force, after all the "legal time," that Howie wasn't as besotted with me as I was with him? Yes, I understood I was not a perfect human—what I was unable to fathom was how I wasn't perfect FOR HIM.

I would not bother to ask Howie these questions or in any way either argue my position or protest his: he said his thing; I saw the world crashing all around his face, just like in that Modern English song, and knew instantly that this was it—we had come to the end. I accepted, with as much grace as I could muster, that any dreams of Howie and I entering our Lunt-Fontanne years or becoming the next Steve and Eydie had been effectively stubbed out, like one of my cigarettes he hated so much because, above all, he was my friend. I will, of course, wonder in that way you do when life deals you a steaming pile of whatthefuckery what might have happened had there been another five performances, or another five weeks of performances, or another five years of performances, or if Howie had been just a tad more open to the idea of me as girlfriend material, or if my self-esteem weren't running on an endless existential Habitrail of self-reproach—would any of it have changed the outcome?

I will ask myself how I could have been so dumb to think that all those times when he was singing the finale to *Pippin* and looking into my eyes, those lyrics were meant for and about me, about us:

> I never came close, my love
> We nearly came near
> It never was there
> I think it was here

Of course it was here—it's always been here—how can he not see this?

Eventually, though, the questions I asked myself would go the way of the questions I'd never asked him—tucked into the untapped treasure trove of acquiescence, only to be exhumed in the future, whenever I hear myself described as "the one that got away."

~

"Look," I told Candace, "there were reasons we never got together when we were younger. And they were not . . . because of me."

Though it was a detail she had theretofore not known, Candace nodded knowingly.

"I get it," she said. "Things are *never* that cut-and-dried."

I told Candace that, in the end, heady though it all was, if I were to jump on a plane to the far-flung Pacific Northwest (or anywhere for that matter), Howie would need to put on his big-boy pants and ask me himself (and lose the blonde because, no).

"I get it," she said again. "AND I couldn't agree with you more. YOU need to feel safe AND you need to hear all this from him."

Candace wasn't just an attaché on a mission—she was also a really good girlfriend.

It was late and we had to get to our next things. Candace flagged down the waiter to pay for our cocktails, and as she did, a tide of emotion swept over the shore of my being.

Was it because of Howie? Thinking about the past? My recently finalized divorce? A kind stranger plying me with hooch?

All of the above?

Who knew, but the lump, which had ebbed and flowed in my throat throughout the span of our hour together, began, once again, to swell.

"I really appreciate you looking out for me," I said. "You're a terrific person."

"Awww," she said, squeezing my hands in hers again, "it's all you, honey!"

I wanted to memorize this holy, fleeting moment, like a pressed wildflower in the pages of my mind: Candace, sitting across from me; the dusty bar light making her aubergine-streaked hair look blue and her features beatific, like Jennifer Jones in *The Song of Bernadette* after the commission determines she really *had* been visited by the Virgin Mary.

"I know it's only been five minutes," I said, "but why do I feel like I've always known you?"

Candace grinned.

"We must have walked through the desert or something," she said, rising from the table and pulling me into a giant hug. "Now listen to me: let's never not hang. And don't be a stranger if you need a shoulder for any reason—'K? I'm yer fan for life . . ."

We said our goodbyes on Eighth Avenue, and Candace disappeared into the rush of theatergoers blowing toward Broadway. As I made my way to dinner, I decided that even if nothing ever came of her assiduous efforts or the evening's revelations, Candace—this fantabulous human gale force who reached out to me through the space-time continuum for no other reason than "just cuz"—was a keeper.

~

A little while later and a few blocks down, I was at Orso with my friend Dean. Every three weeks or so Dean and I got together for dinner to dish the latest-and-greatest news of the Great White Way. I always looked forward to these meals; Dean, a brilliant theater producer, was one of those friends whose every word you hang on and to whom you are generally only willing to say goodbye when you look around to note that you are the only ones left in the joint and the waitstaff is yawning. But on this night, despite the fact that we had lots to discuss, including Dean's forthcoming Broadway show, I was unable to focus on anything but what had just transpired at the Russian Samovar. My physical body might have been feasting on *fegato e cipolle*, but my mind was hurtling back across the decades to begin a sweeping overview of what had happened between Howie and me.

Life went on and so did we and so, by the way, did *Almost Romance*, but with movie stars in our roles because apparently even playing fictional paramours was no longer in the cards for us. Howie graduated, and then a year later I did too, and even after the whole Elephant & Castle kibosh, we not only stayed friends, but everything remained pretty much status quo.

Howie would write a play; he'd come over to my place in the Village with said play; he'd listen while I read all the parts aloud at my dining table; we'd adjourn to the sofa for what can only be described as not-even-remotely-legal-time; he'd go back to his apartment in Brooklyn and Talia, the Canadian RA.

For some reason, this arrangement, which lasted for about three years, struck me as fine, or let's say fine-*ish*. I didn't want him out of my life entirely, so I settled—something, when it comes to love, at which I would become particularly adept. Feasting on the crumbs, as my shrink would later opine. But I didn't see it that way—not then. In fact, at some point, I got to feeling pretty grand, telling myself that because we were never boyfriend and girlfriend, we could never break up, so maybe I got "forever" after all. It would be grossly untrue to say that never once before, during, or after those assignations did I yearn for anything more or feel used or bummed or otherwise take personally what I came to view as an immense failure of imagination on his part, because *of course I did*. But I became expert at batting those feelings away just as soon as they arose. I'd practice not paying too-too much heed to thoughts akin to the card-shark axiom my former teacher David Mamet used to repeat, "You can't win if you don't play." Instead, I simply made the choice to believe that we *were* winning—we got to have the best of each other but none of the worst.

Then came the day that all the amorphousness came to an end: it was 1990; Howie's girlfriend Talia had gone to Kripalu for a few months and came home so ashram-ed that the relationship, or what was left of it, was over. But something else had happened during the interim: I'd fallen in love. Even though my initial attraction to my new jazz musician boyfriend was that he had "a Howie vibe," I was now madly in love *with him* and not at all interested in anyone else. This was relayed to Howie one late night at David's Pot Belly (the Christopher Street haunt where the baked-egg casserole concoctions with a side of "potato balls" were the stuff of legends) in the midst of discussing David Lean's newly restored *Lawrence of Arabia*. I remember saying how taken I was with Omar Sharif's breathtaking entrance in which he appears out of a mirage on his camel; how once he arrives, Lawrence's life is changed forever, while Howie, on the other hand, was obsessed with another Omar moment, the one where he says, "For some men, nothing is written unless they write it."

And just when he was pointing out that even if there's fate or destiny, there's *also* such a thing as free will, *it's all in your hands*, he grabbed MY hand across the table, and that's when I did something I'd never done before: I pulled it away.

Dun-dun-dun.

"I'm in love," I told him, "and this isn't cool anymore."

And not only was hand-holding not cool anymore, but any sort of post-snack make-out sesh wasn't cool anymore either. In the future, when reminded of this incident, Howie will not only have zero recall of the venerated David's Pot Belly, he will not remember the "potato balls." And this is not a person who forgets a potato very easily, you understand—this is a person who considers potatoes to be not just "nature's perfect food" but some of the best friends he's ever had. Now, while Howie's emotional amnesia will delete this moment from his mind forever, it was as vivid to me twenty-five years later as Dean and the plate of *fegato e cipolle* I had barely touched.

There I was, waxing poetic about my new beau's many charms, while Howie sat across from me, pissed and petulant, dousing his potato balls with ketchup until they, too, were drowning in his gratuitous gobs of self-pity. For the first time ever, though, I didn't care. Howie might have still had feelings for me that veered between mad passion and ambivalence; mine for him, however, had been shaped by several years of rejections and push-pulls and self-centered opportunism. *Let him be petty and ungenerous*, I thought to myself, *things have been "fluid" long enough*. I was so over playing "tart with a heart" Belle Watling to his rascally Rhett Butler—I deserved more than "legal time" with someone who'd never love me for real—and now, at long last, I had it with someone else, so fuck Howie and the potato he rode in on.

Well.

I assumed, just like I had after that fateful day at Elephant & Castle, that *that* would be *that*, and the David's Pot Belly repast would hammer the final nail in the Nancy-Howie coffin.

But then, a funny thing happened.

About a week after David's Pot Belly, Howie left a message on my answering machine:

> *Hey, it's me. So there's this new movie out called* Tie Me Up! Tie Me Down! *playing right down the street from you at the Cinema Village. It's from . . . Spain, I guess? Anyway, it's s'pposedly a romantic comedy about a newly released mental patient who kidnaps an actress to make her fall in love with him. NOW, you're an actress and I often behave like a mental patient, so this feels very us, BUT, unlike the movie, I will not try to make you do anything (except probably explain the movie to me cuz this shit sounds bananas)—I KNOW YOU HAVE A BOYFRIEND! AND I'M VERY HAPPY FOR YOU! I'm sorry I was a dick the other week. Call me!*

So we go to the movie and we go as legit friends—no canoodling, no fondling, no hand-holding, and all of a sudden, guess what else is missing? *Tension.* All the tension, the frustration, the endless expectations, the *will we, won't we, does he, doesn't he, is she, isn't she*—all gone. And in its place the pure, unadulterated joy of two fledgling barely-out-of-their-teens souls realizing that quitting the hanky-panky didn't necessitate quitting *each other*. The ineffable spark that existed from that first moment at the Brittany message desk needn't be extinguished, nor could it be; instead, it paved the way to a new, deeper level of friendship.

A few months after we see the sexually twisted movie about the actress and the mental patient, Howie goes on a first date with a woman to see *Misery*, the Stephen King movie about a writer saved by a woman who turns out to be psychotic and then tortures him. Maybe it was because he didn't have to read subtitles, but something about that paradigm must have felt more right to him, because within a year they were engaged. But seriously—this chick was very cool and she and I became friends, even hanging out sans Howie.

Almost Romance's off-Broadway run begot Howie's first television writing gig; he thereupon moved to Los Angeles, got married; then I moved to Los Angeles, got married; then Howie had a kid and got divorced; then I moved back to New York, had a kid, and got divorced. And over the course of those twenty-five years, Howie and I became each other's best buds, sounding boards, support systems, lifelines, amateur shrinks, and reality checks.

Who was the person I told about being repeatedly sexually harassed by my acting teacher, and who was the *only* person who made me feel like, *no*, it actually *wasn't* my fault? Who was the person he called to help him obtain his International Bartending School diploma in case his writing aspirations didn't pan out? (ME: "How do you make a gin and tonic?" HIM: BLANK STARE. ME: "I know you can do it." HIM: BLANK STARE. ME: "The clue is *in the name*.")

Who did *he* call first when his spouse announced she was leaving him? Who did *I* call first when I decided to leave mine?

This is not to say that my best bud was perfect—he wasn't. He could be impatient, arrogant, competitive; he saw me expansively but also, at times, narrowly—not unlike how he saw himself. But for the majority of my life, he was the person with whom I could dialogue about all the parts I otherwise felt too ashamed of—my breakups, fuckups, failings, and flailings—and it was like conferring with the wisest part of myself: the part that would always say, *Yeah, but*, when I felt finished; the part that saw blue skies where I saw a tempest; the part that could always, *always* find the funny.

After the dinner I didn't eat, Dean and I ordered some mint tea I didn't drink, and as Orso began to fill with the after-theater crowd, I found myself transported to another restaurant, this one thirty blocks down and ten springs earlier.

Postpartum, post-realizing my marriage is likely beyond repair, I see myself, a mass of moroseness in the Meatpacking District, sitting across from Howie, who has come to town to see theater, to see me, and to meet my baby girl. It is the latest in a lifetime of lunches that stretch languidly across an afternoon into an early evening wherein we dissect anything and everything that needs dissecting. We talk about our careers, my new daughter, his new girlfriend. There are, of course, burgers and fries and the requisite *extra-extra* ketchup on the side, followed by a sundae with *extra-extra* hot fudge on the side, because sauce to sauce people is a source of both pleasure and solace.

"So, what else?" he asks. "Are you writing?"

"Yes," I say. "Trying."

"Nothing's clean and easy. Look, I know you're depressed. I get it. I've been there. Just remember that thing Vonnegut said, 'God never wrote a perfect scene.'"

"I barely recognize myself anymore."

"Well, your old pal How recognizes you. And can I just say, not for nothin': You. Look. Stunning!"

"I look like shit."

"Excuse me, but has there ever been a more smokin'-hot, post-preggo chick? Lady? MILF? By the way, is 'MILF' out now?"

"It was never in."

"OK, well, jeez," he says, "you know me—always a disaster when I try to be hip." He makes a jazz-hands-y gesture, then realizes he's made a jazz-hands-y gesture. "Ya like my jazz hands?"

Our friendship, our sauces, our hangs—I cling to them all like a sandbar in a riptide.

"Oh, Howie. I dunno what the fuck to do. I gotta pull my ass out of the ash can cuz . . . I seriously hate everything in my life right now. Except my baby . . . and the fact that because of her I'm finally a C cup."

"Ya know something," he says, "at the end of the day, whenever you're bummed, think about how much you love your new boobs—BABY! BABY! I MEANT BABY!"

At this, we roar with laughter. We laugh and laugh and laugh, and the two of us are howling so hard over this stupid not-so-Freudian slip that we can barely breathe. Not since *Match Game* '76 have any two people laughed so hard over the word "boobs."

"How come I knew you'd be as excited about my new knockers as I am?"

"Cuz you know me," he says.

"You're seriously the only person who could make me laugh right now."

He nods.

"Cuz *I* know *you.*"

Later, when he emails me from LA, he will reiterate the Vonnegut thing; he will encourage me to "write your way out of the ash can." *I have missed the living fuck outta you, Nance,* he will write. *I seriously cannot go so long without seeing or at least talking to you—you're way too important to me. Please don't forget that.*

~

There was still a nip in the air as Dean and I said our goodbyes on Forty-Sixth Street, but I decided to walk the twentysomething blocks home. What with the sudsy bubble bath of memories flooding the floor of my consciousness, I felt plenty toasty in my wool-gathering cocoon, floating my way through Hell's Kitchen. Song after song played on my iPhone, and yet it was Howie's words via Candace that gushed through my headphones:

"There was always more . . ."
"Shimmering thread . . ."
"The truth is, I'm in love with her . . ."

I was souped-up on *l'amour*, afire with the flames of fantasy—nothing could kill my buzz.

But somewhere between Hudson Yards and Chelsea, the love loop was supplanted by some *other* words heard earlier that evening:

Eh, she lives in New York; I live in LA . . .

She's got a kid; I've got a kid . . .

It's a good story, but . . .

[RECORD SCRATCH.]

And suddenly I realized, *Oh my god—he's right*: it's a good *story*. STO-RY.

This isn't real life, I thought to myself. It's not *even close* to real life.

And let's face it—when you get right down to it, it's not even really *a story*. It's more like a series of half-baked plot points cooked up by writers trying to curry favor with their boss while waiting for their next snack break. I thought about all the shit that gave me pause—the public airing of my private email, for instance, and what about Candace and her "If you don't marry this woman, I will"—could I really be a sucker for such blandishments? The snarl of ingredients that made up the evening's strange soup continued to swirl, and the more it did, the more I was like: What the hell was I thinking? That I'm in one of those nineties Meg Ryan confections and I'm Meg Ryan? *Meg Ryan* isn't even Meg Ryan anymore! There's a reason why romantic comedies are "boy-meets-girl" and not "middle-aged-bald-guy-finally-decides-to-give-it-a-go-with-perimenopausal-pal," and that's because "boys and girls" don't have complicated lives with kids and joint-custody agreements stipulating that they can't leave the five boroughs of New York City. I might have been a "free woman" with a career as portable as my laptop, but that didn't mean I was free to up and move to California. And Howie, what with a Los Angeles–based TV show and teenage son, wasn't about to swap coasts either. What possessed me to get so carried away, so ridiculously enthusiastic, so enthusy-woozy? Talk about the power of suggestion; talk about hope and its eternal springs. "You need to hear all this from him," she'd said. Well, yeah, *but I didn't*, and you know something, maybe I won't.

"Maybe you won't," my neighbor Nat concurred after I got home and ran through the aforementioned litany. Nat was babysitting the Bear that night (along with his partner, Troy, who'd long gone to bed), and had been waiting with bated breath to debrief me about my mystery meeting. For the next hour or so, I told him all about Howie and our history and Candace Kahn and her play and the Russian Samovar and the writers' room and the Darth Vader email and the Blonde Nobody Likes. Yes, I told him, I do still have feelings for Howie and there's always been this *thing* and I've wondered and he's wondered and now it seems like a bevy of people I don't even know are wondering—

Nat raised his hand.

"Yes?"

"I'm wondering . . ."

"Right," I laughed, "now *you're* wondering—everybody's wondering! Wondering abounds! But, you know, what I'm *really* wondering is, if Howie and I harbored such intensely amorous feelings toward one other, what's prevented us, in the four years since my marriage ended, from exploring any sort of romantic relationship? And I mean *really* exploring? I mean, OK, my divorce was only finalized two months ago, BUT *before that* I was separated for four fucking years—how is it that we never gave 'it' a go?

"But, you know something," I continued, "maybe it wasn't s'pposed to happen. I don't subscribe to the theory that 'everything happens for a reason' (I used to but don't anymore); I do, however, believe that certain things DON'T happen for a reason—"

"So do I—"

"And maybe Howie and I together is one of them."

Nat nodded.

"Maybe," I pressed on, "the best love affairs are the ones that remain in the realm of fantasy. Maybe existing, as Howie put it, 'on the periphery,' as opposed to in the crux, is the secret to an enduring romance. Or the secret to ours, which was never really a romance at all—just an 'almost.'"

Nat nodded again. He got me. He always got me. And more than that he understood what I did: that some territories are better left uncharted.

"And now," Nat said, rising to leave, "we gotta figure out how to get you to Oregon."

PART TWO

London Terrace

April 25–June 12, 2015

As I was most days, the morning after the Samovar, I was roused to consciousness by Teddy Pendergrass:
Wake up, everybody, no more sleepin' in bed
No more backward thinkin' time for thinkin' ahead . . .
Though it's generally a really lovely way to be spirited from slumber, on this day I arose with not just Teddy and his raspy baritone but a hangover and, more pressingly, a mandate:

DO. NOT. GET. SUCKED. INTO. FANTASY.

After which I spent the rest of the day getting, more or less, sucked into fantasy.

In truth, some of it was sanctioned; the evening before had been, after all, pretty heady. To expect I'd not indulge in even a smidge of fancy . . . well, let's just say I knew that attempting to adhere to such stringency would be at best unrealistic and at worst more onerous than Dry January.

Nat's Oregon comment as the evening's capper hadn't helped, though I knew not to take *it* or *him* too-too seriously. Here was a guy whose entire MO seemed at times to be solely devoted to getting his girlfriends gainfully affianced. You'd think a man of such cultivated élan and mordant wit would have better things to do with his energy, but no. If Nat thought a hubby might be in the offing for one of his ladies, he'd turn on a dime from a *de nos jours* Noël Coward to Barbara Stanwyck as the brassy, down-on-her-heels mother in *Stella Dallas*, endlessly sacrificing her daughter's way to a more bourgeois life.

Anyway, I knew myself. Too much of a rebel.

The type of person who only hankers for the verboten.

The type of person who the minute there's a dietary restriction openly devours an entire box of chocolates.

The type of person who has no interest in the sun unless, of course, there's an eclipse.

You get the picture.

Given the aforementioned, I felt it best to allow myself the day to enjoy, without censure, thinking about whatever the fuck I wanted to think about. Not every moment, you understand—I had shit to do—but, within the scope of my myriad activities, I figured, why not allow myself to daydream about Nancy and Howie, or to portmanteau us, "Nowie"? Why not every so often wade into that particular pool for a little swim, steep myself in what had been, splash around in what could be, get it out of my system, and move on?

The Bear's sitter Kajsa came by to take her to art class; I, meanwhile, hustled myself down to Caffe Dante in the Village, first to meet with a magazine editor with whom I'd been freelancing, then to spend the next few hours working on the book proposal that needed to be off my desk and onto my agent's by Monday morning. I loved my Saturdays at Dante. I generally don't like writing in public, what with all the noise and distractions, but Dante was different: not so busy you can't think; busy enough so you're sufficiently stimulated. It was the place I liked to go when stuck or otherwise demoralized by the writing process, to "trick myself" into making headway. I liked to call it "self-ruse-Saturday": "Oh, no, no, no—I'm not *really writing*," the gambit would go, "I'm just chillin' amid the hubbub, *jotting . . .*"

The other thing about Caffe Dante was that it was the perfect place to toil on Saturdays when the Bear, out of school and with a sitter, would otherwise be in my midst, and on that particular Saturday, when I needed to produce pages while my mind was rife with "Nowie," there was the added bonus of being down in the Village, where our story began. Interspersed with arranging, then rearranging, words and sentences, I was like, *Did he really say those things about me to his writing staff—these total strangers (to me anyway)?! Or was it all just hyperbole? Whatevs, even if he did say it, even if he means it, even if he were to reach out—then what?*

"Shimmering thread" . . . *I love that.*

*I love being described as "shimmering" anything. Am I always shimmering? Like, are you only shimmering in the eyes of another or does a person just invariably, unimpeachably shimmer? It's not a thing you could put on your LinkedIn, but a thing nonetheless, right? And speaking of things, he's **in a** thing, yes? Which, even if he's not, or they break up or whatever, he's either in a thing or five seconds out of a thing and, honestly, I can't. I'm too old to be cleanup batter (not that I was ever young enough to be cleanup batter), and OMG, here I go with the sports metaphors—I don't even like sports, but somehow I'm always employing them, which, now that I think about it, is a thing Howie always loved.* "Wait!" *I remember him once exclaiming over chicken burgers in the nineties.* "Did you literally just call eating shrimp at a Reform Jewish wedding a 'flagrant foul'? I FUCKING LOOOOOVE when you get all sporty. It's like eating lunch with an insanely hot combo of Bob Costas and Isaac Bashevis Singer!"

Anyway. As has been discussed, we live in different places, as far apart as you can physically get on mainland soil. Two ships passing in the night, never the twain shall meeting up every so often as friends, usually when one or both of our romantic entanglements has blown to smithereens, asking ourselves or each other why we'd never given "us" a go. Clinically, as if trying to unravel mysterious characters we'd seen on the page or the stage, we'd posit explanations—ones that made sense, were logical, well reasoned, clear-eyed, whathaveyou—that no matter what, never seemed to quell or satisfy the compulsion to ask the same fucking question over and over again, ad infinitum.

*Also, and not for nothing, even if I'm available, am I **really** available? I'm not so sure. Sometimes I feel like my romantic history is an especially robust pupu platter of WTF. And, you know something, maybe it's me. Maybe I'm just incapable of compatibility. Whatever. All I know is that as of now I have three, maybe four, new magazine assignments to file and a finished book proposal, all of which will be going out in the next month, and for the rest of today I get to be "shimmering" . . .*

At the finish of a Dante sesh, usually around three or four, I grab a coffee to go and, if the weather's good, walk the mile and a half home. That Saturday, I lingered a bit in Washington Square Park. I always loved these moments of springtime in the City when, after a brutal and unforgiving winter, everyone from the curmudgeonly to the supercalifragilistic has slithered their way out of their burrows to frolic once more in the sun. I pass the guy in the dress playing upright piano; a jazz octet under the arch; bums sleeping on benches; coeds draped around each other, around the fountain, around an activist, around a juggler. Everything looked exactly as it did in the heyday of "Nowie." It wasn't the styles that made you know it was late April 2015, but the technology: no one was fiddling with a cellular device in the eighties. And yet, if I squinted, if I ignored the hands and faces Velcroed to phones, I could almost pretend it wasn't now but then and see "Nowie"—chatting, laughing, a bundle of late-adolescent energy, bravado, and ideas—in each and every tableau.

From the park I ambled through the West Village to Gansevoort Street, making my way, finally, onto the High Line, the once-dilapidated elevated rail line repurposed, thanks to urban renewal, into a greenway that stretches a mile and a half along the west side of Manhattan.

It took a bit longer, but whether it was post-school drop-offs, or after my Saturdays at Dante, something about wending my way home via the herbaceous fantasia of the High Line exfoliated the granular detritus of my soul. Just a few blocks past Chelsea Market, the one-time Nabisco factory where, a hundred years before, the Oreo cookie was hatched, the original train tracks become visible between the dogwoods, bottlebrush, and hollies and you can almost get a sense of how Chelsea used to look when it was just a forest of farmland and apple orchards built up by robber barons. But the best part of all is just past Eighteenth Street, when what becomes finally visible, amid a thicket of dense shrubs and trees, marrying the industrial to the vegetal, is the mythical London Terrace Gardens, rising directly to the north like a citadel.

"In your life there are a few places," Alice Munro once wrote, "or maybe only the one place, where something happened, and then there are all the other places." That place for me was London Terrace Gardens, the greatest place in a city of great places.

Even before I ever lived there I had heard the apocryphal tale that if you are a gay man living in New York City, you will, at some point, sleep with someone who lives in London Terrace Gardens. But what I hadn't known, until I was in the throes of my divorce, was that there was another rumor about my West Chelsea apartment building, and this one wasn't quite so auspicious. This one held that if a heterosexual couple makes their home at London Terrace, the male will eventually skedaddle while the female (and their issue) will remain on the premises, in some cases, forever. In other words: what's good for the gander(s) was a shit show for the goose.

I first heard about my building's supposed malediction one night when my neighbor Jenna Ferrer from the eighth floor had come up to my apartment on the tenth for a glass of wine. I was remarking on how weird it was that so many marriages in our building had ended up in Splitsville and, further, how in every instance I could think of it was the man who had moved out and moved on while the woman stayed—and stayed single to boot.

"It's as if this place is cursed," I said, laughing.

"Well, that's because it is," said Jenna, not laughing at all. "That's what people say, anyway."

"What people?"

"People—anyone who knows. It's Terrace lore."

And then, for the next forty-five minutes, I sat riveted as Jenna explained how it was that our place of abode had become such conjugal kryptonite. It seemed that the guy who owned the property back in the late twenties had a vision of developing a group of row houses that took up two city blocks into the largest luxury building in New York City. Within a few years, his dream was realized: one thousand apartments, connected by two courtyard English gardens and boasting a surfeit of "modern" conveniences like a post office, an Olympic-size swimming pool, a gymnasium, and a full-service garage. There were doormen at every entrance, costumed in British Bobby getups, and the camp even extended to Christmas parties replete with Babe Ruth—in full Santa-drag—passing out gifts.

Then, after a few years, the stock market crashed. London Terrace went into default, and the despondent developer, millions of dollars in debt, climbed to the top of his creation and leapt to his death. Legend had it that the developer's tragic end caused a ripple effect that would mean heartbreak to generations of straight women residents and non-stop booty calls for the gay male ones. Lesbians, apparently, would remain untouched.

"Years ago," Jenna continued, "at the end of a serious relationship, a friend bought me a session with a well-regarded healer—you know, a person who comes over to clear out any sort of negative energy by, like, burning sage for an hour or so. Anyway, she comes over—she's very nice, this woman, doesn't look weird at all—sort of like Katie Couric in a caftan—she does my apartment, which was all fine, but then, at the end, she says, 'I'm still feeling sadness.' So we go on a hunt through the building—up and down stairwells, through the lobby and various hallways, so she could, like, ferret out where this 'sadness' was coming from. Anyway, somehow, we ended up in the north courtyard and she zeros in on it there, in one of the flower beds that rim the edge."

"What did that mean? Why was the 'sadness' there?"

Jenna looked at me.

"Maybe that's where he, you know, *landed*," she said, quietly.

I sat for a moment, thinking about the courtyard, how despite its beauty it wasn't especially inviting and that no one ever seemed compelled to hang out there. I always figured it was because you weren't allowed to take your dog in there, but maybe it had more to do with the sad flower beds?

I thought about the women in the building I knew whose relationships had tanked. There was, of course, Jenna, who, despite the healer's best efforts, hadn't been with a man since her last breakup. There was my downstairs neighbor Susie Jacobs, the hoarder with a heart of gold, and my upstairs neighbor the Italian fashion editor—both beautiful, both serially jilted. There was my dope-ass single-working-mom posse: Bibi Carrasquillo, on the seventh floor, whose ex had been a porn/drug/gambling addict, and Dorie Katz from the sixth floor, whose ex had practically bankrupted her. There was my thrice-divorced eighty-six-year-old down-the-hall neighbor, Rosalie, who'd lived in London Terrace since 1963; there was Lola Pacino, a supposed cousin of Al, who'd had at least two marriages that failed and a string of live-ins who now lived out; the woman from the sixteenth floor with the frizzy hair, whose name I can never remember, who used to be married to the Japanese guy. Me.

"What about that British couple?" I asked. "You know, the ones with the two kids named after Orwellian characters and the husband had something to do with *Mob Wives*?"

Jenna shook her head.

"They moved out," she said.

"They did?"

"Years ago—"

"Just in the nick of time, apparently—"

"And anyway, they were never married—remember? They were socialists . . ."

I sat for a second, thinking.

"Judith and Ari!" I said, jumping up like I was on a game show.

"You didn't hear?" Jenna said, arching her brow.

"Hear what?" I asked, sinking back to my losing seat on the sofa.

"Done," Jenna said, over-enunciating the *D* and the *N*. "Ari moved out last Tuesday."

"No way," I gasped.

"Way. And Judith can't afford to stay; she and Milo are going to have to move in with her parents in Jersey."

I was starting to feel a bit like Carol Kane in *When a Stranger Calls*, when the cops tell her the calls are coming from *inside* the house. Still, I had some questions: Didn't a curse usually bear some sort of direct or, at the very least, *thematic* connection to the, um . . . accursed? What was the correlation between some dude's rotten business luck and the love lives of women in our building?

"Maybe he was just a garden-variety misogynist," Jenna laughed. "They generally don't need much of a reason."

"You don't really believe it, do you?" I asked Jenna as we sipped the last of our wine.

"Don't ask me," she laughed. "I'm a half-Irish, half–Puerto Rican lapsed Catholic, which makes me a hundred percent superstitious."

This was true: Years before, Jenna was walking home from work in SoHo one night when she saw a large painting in a gallery window. Cubist, done in the fifties by a noted female artist, it was a stunningly moody portrait of a woman in dishabille, seated on a chair. She loved it. It wasn't in her budget, but the gallerist agreed to let Jenna put it on lay-away. After a year of monthly payments, the day finally came when the painting was hers. Jenna was overjoyed, carrying it by herself, through the bustling streets of SoHo, all the way home, like Jill Clayburgh at the end of *An Unmarried Woman*. For years it hung over her bed. That is, until the "healer" showed up.

"She said it had negative energy," Jenna said. "And having it in my bedroom *especially* was keeping men away."

Jenna wasn't sure she believed her, but like the curse, she wasn't sure she *didn't* believe her either. So down it came, the painting she'd so pined for, around which the decor of her bedroom had been designed. With nowhere suitable to hang it—she had other walls, obviously, but where, exactly, does one hang a giant (naked) Fuck You to men—and because she couldn't bear to sell it, Jenna carefully covered the painting and stuck it in the back of her coat closet.

"Maybe it's ridiculous," Jenna said, "but my attitude was why risk it? I mean, at some point, I'd at least like to go on a date."

As amusing as it was to imagine the same freethinking dwelling that housed a punk-rock pioneer, an avant-garde essayist, and the guy who invented the Cosmo was also harboring a super-sexist supernatural, not all the neighbors were so tickled. Dorie Katz, for instance, objected to the mere mention of our supposed hetero-hazardous-hex, insisting that its very underpinnings were rooted in tired chauvinistic tropes designed to perpetuate the systemic oppression of women.

"Who comes up with this crap—Norman Mailer?" she smirked as we stood one evening in the laundry room, folding sheets and clothes, along with Bibi Carrasquillo.

"Right?" Bibi laughed. "So ridic—"

"I build not one but two successful businesses after my bum-of-an-ex left me with debt up to my *pupik* and a toddler to support," Dorie continued, "but somehow *I'm* cursed cuz *he's* gone?"

"I won't lie," Bibi said. "I was devastated at first, but now that I'm outta the drama of *that* shitty relationship? Some curse," she cackled. "I've never felt so lucky!"

Right on. Sisters are doin' it (yes, that included the laundry) for themselves. While generally speaking, my credulity in the paranormal ran more to Jenna's and my politics to Dorie's and Bibi's, it was hard to get worked up either way about the place I came to view as my port in the storm.

That said, there was always something just a tad otherworldly to me about London Terrace Gardens, a place I'd heard about for years before I'd ever stepped past its gryphon-festooned entry. It was one of those rarest of urban jewels, the kind spoken about in hushed tones: a fabled fortress of faded glamour and eccentric denizens; rent-stabilized, pet-friendly, and with a normally yearslong waitlist. The rent included heat, electricity, hot water, and security. There was the aforementioned pool. But, at the time London Terrace came into my life, I didn't care about any of that; I needed a place in a jiffy, one that was affordable and had walls. My husband and I had been living in a one-room loft that was inconveniently bohemian and even more inconveniently expensive, and at the same time, we were expecting a baby and unexpectedly no longer getting along. Glancing at the *Times* Real Estate section one morning, a listing caught my eye for a one-bedroom at the "downtown Dakota," and though morning sickness had me in peak-puke mode, I decided to stagger up Ninth Avenue to have a look. I would later feel it was providence that sent me—pregnant and desperate at the end of the lease on my overpriced rental and at the end of my tether with my unhappy marriage—to check out a listing that, according to the management office, had never been placed.

What ad? We don't even list vacancies in the paper . . .

Fortunately, whatever psychic glitch caused the phantom listing to appear in my preggo-brain had also put me in line to be the first to know that a different unit, one on a higher floor and with a tiny slip of an Empire State Building view, had opened up the day before.

Would you like to have a look?

Five minutes later, I stood in its sun-dappled living room, gazing out the double-hung windows at the blanket of ivy growing up the redbrick exterior wall across the courtyard. It was one of those late-June Sundays when everything is suddenly abloom, and something about those leaves waving languidly in the breeze, as if conducting Beethoven's *Pastoral*, made me feel like this would be an OK perch for a minute. Or at least until we figured out the things we could not yet figure out. I'd spend the next thirteen autumns watching those leaves turn from green to red to orange to yellow to brown before vanishing completely until some late-June Sunday, when all at once the verdant fantasia would be magically restored. I couldn't imagine then, as I stood there, leaning into the transitory, how different it would all look in a few months, how different *I* would look in a few months; let alone how different everything would be thirteen leaf rotations later. Just as I could not have anticipated the ways in which the ivy's steadfast regeneration would inspire my own.

The biggest surprise, however, was the intense ardor I would come to feel for London Terrace. Despite a rental rate that went from the sublime to the ridiculous; despite bitter, ever-roiling issues between tenants and management (the blight of malevolent New York City real estate forces), by the time I'd learned about my building's supposed affliction, I not only loved living there, I loved living there more than anywhere I'd ever lived. It was my baby's first home, the place to which her father and I brought her following her arrival one blustery February morning; the place where she received the honorific "Boo Boo Bear." It was the place where, after my dog and my marriage died, the Bear and I and our Burmese cat, Fosse, figured out how to live, despite our bereavement and perennially low funds, in style. It was also the place where, in a closet, I learned to write; the place where, in a shitty little kitchen, I learned to cook; the place about which I'd originally felt kind of meh, then fought like hell to keep; the place that kept *me* when I felt expendable and broken beyond repair.

Above all, though, it was the place where I came to know some of the most significant people of my adult life, neighbors who became friends, who then became more family than family. New York City can be an alienating place of shaky connections, its inhabitants, even on the best of days, cold, brusque, in a hurry. I have lived in apartment buildings where residents sharing the same elevator every day for years and years never traded even cursory eye contact, let alone words, preferring instead to direct their undivided focus to the floor indicator with the laser-like intensity of a glassblower. You didn't take it personally; it was just the way things were in a city filled with noise and soot and proximity, where everyone was trying to carve out their own corner of quiet.

But London Terrace was a different vibe, its own animal, the kind you "rescue" only to realize later the creature has, in fact, saved *you*. It was where the Bear and I one day struck up a conversation with Jenna in the elevator that turned into dinner; where lingering in the lobby, enveloped in *gemütlichkeit*, we met Dorie, whose office off the lobby sat alongside offices for both a doula and an "urban shaman"; the same lobby where we were befriended by Bibi one day and then Paulie the Pothead, who rescued old Great Danes and young street hustlers, the next. It was where we attended our downstairs neighbor Susie's Shabbats and seders and jewelry trunk shows and even senatorial fundraisers; where we began looking after our elderly, addled, down-the-hall neighbor, Rosalie. It was where the Bear and I began to entertain, and not just slapdash, you understand, but in the grandest of manners, behaving as if our one-bedroom apartment was the height of haute interiors and we were the Elsa Maxwells of modern downtown. Soirees for award shows, birthdays, holidays, movie screenings to which all our neighbors came, even the ones allergic to Fosse, to dine, to watch, to cuddle with us on our lumpy leopard-print sofa.

It was where, also, one Saturday morning in the new coffee shop installed in the bottom of the building, the Bear spotted a beautiful, fortyish, ex-Kansas farm-boy-turned-makeup-artist named Troy, whose leopard Louboutin sneakers looked remarkably similar to the sale-rack H&M ones gracing her own feet. "I like your sneakers," she told him as we stood in line for her hot chocolate.

"Well, I like *your* sneakers," he said, winking, thus igniting one of the greatest soul connections in the history of love. After a "first date" wherein Troy and his partner, Nat, and the Bear and I trooped up to see a remastered print of the Audrey Hepburn–Fred Astaire jeu d'esprit *Funny Face* on the big screen at Lincoln Center, we not only never went back to *before*—the four of us could no longer even remember that one existed. Our page one began as if there was no backstory at all, as if there was never a time when Troy, Nat, the Bear, and I were *not* seeing each other every day, sometimes several times a day, rushing across the City to Shake Shack or tiny French bakeries or the Big Gay Ice Cream shop for "Salty Pimps" and "Bea Arthur" cones. Never a time before "the Boys," as we came to call them, were my co-parents, taking the Bear to museums and fashion exhibits and to get her ears pierced at Claire's on Eighty-First Street. Never a time before the hot-pink Martha Stewart tissue-paper disco balls were festooned above the Bear's bed or when people were gasping over the deftly art-directed-within-an-inch-of-their-lives Halloween costumes that turned the Bear into Audrey Hepburn in *Breakfast at Tiffany's*, Madonna circa "Borderline," and Liz Taylor's *Cleopatra*.

We had each other's keys and we had each other's backs at London Terrace. Occasionally, we even had each other's vodka, like the Christmas I was hosting a dinner and ran out of liquor, then helped myself to the

Stoli I knew my neighbors, Bruce and Todd—who were away skiing—had stored in their freezer. That I not only had carte blanche to Bruce and Todd's home but knew the contents of their fridge (and that they wouldn't mind; they'd only laugh at me for running out of booze in the first place) was only remarkable in how utterly unremarkable it really was. But that's what it was like living at London Terrace Gardens: ours was not just the usual coexisting-in-shoeboxes-high-in-the-sky but something out of place and time, like the mythical village in *Brigadoon* or a modern shtetl—an urban Anatevka (with doormen), perhaps—populated by the most caring, generous, nosy, judgy, perfectly imperfect collection of humans with whom you could ever be hashtag-blessed to get stuck in a cursed building.

Life was by no means flawless; there were still things to aspire to, but for once I was at peace with the process instead of perpetually ruing it. I wasn't even ashamed of whatever had or hadn't happened in my life as I'd been so many times before, not after Troy and Nat hipped me to *kintsugi*—the Japanese art of repairing broken pottery in which the piece is mended with golden glue so that the breakage remains visible. The point of this, they told me, is that the history of the object, what it's been through, is to be celebrated as opposed to disguised. After a lifetime of feeling duty bound to conceal life's blemishes, to emotionally (or medicinally) Botox the wrinkles, I waved a hearty ha-ha to both societal compulsions and my own self-deprecations. I was kintsugi. My breakage henceforth emblazoned in gold. And curse or no curse, I'd found my tribe.

~

An entirely different curse, one of the star-crossed variety, was on my mind when on Friday, May 8, I received an email from Netflix:

"Nancy," trumpets the cheery subject line, "we just added a TV show you might like!"

A glossy photo heralding the premiere of *Grace and Frankie* ensued, featuring a glamorously vexed Jane Fonda shrugging off an adorably vex-*ing* Lily Tomlin. The email felt both Big Brother–y in its targeting (*clearly*, someone had kept an assiduous accounting of my many wine-soaked *First Wives Club* viewings) and stalker-y (um . . . did Netflix know I know Howie?). It had been two weeks since my Dirty Martinis with Candace; two weeks since the "Nowie" wave crested and began its gradual wane and the zesty waters of intrigue had wound their way down to placid once more. I'd not heard a peep from Howie, not that I *really* thought I would, especially as time moved further and further from the Samovar summit. The truth was, though, I felt just fine about it. More than fine. In fact, the prevailing feeling coursing through my being was one of relief. I had for the first time in a very long time achieved a level of tranquility: my divorce was finally in the rearview mirror; career-wise, I was cooking with gas; the life the Bear and I had built since the split was full and, at least to us, fabulous; and something about this particular amalgam made the idea of introducing anything new into the mix feel a tad too rock-the-boat-ish. That said, tormented though our relationship at times had seemed, Howie was and would always be one of my most treasured pals, and I wouldn't have missed the debut of his career's high point for anything.

"Are we gonna watch Howie's show tonight?" the Bear had asked over breakfast.

"Yup," I said. "We can start watching when you get home from school this afternoon."

"YAYYYYYYYY!" she cried. "HOW-EEE!"

She didn't really know Howie, she just worshipped him, or rather his work, from afar. Anytime she saw his name in the credits of whatever show he happened to be working on, she'd leap from her seat on the sofa, arms flung triumphantly in the air like someone had just scored a touchdown, and shriek: "HOW-EEE!"

I tried to imagine them together, what that would be like. *I dunno,* I thought to myself. Anytime a dude seemed to be even remotely flirty with me, she hadn't exactly cottoned to it. I mean, a guy got within five hundred paces and my normally delightful child became a cockblock extraordinaire. Once, when we ran into this playwright I know and as he was chatting me up, the Bear decided she'd had enough and asked if she could lie down . . . IN THE MIDDLE OF SIXTH AVENUE. Another time, at an avant-garde circus in Brooklyn, as the gentleman sitting next to us tried to woo me into visiting his "Japanese/Italian-fusion restaurant in Dumbo," the Bear insisted his eatery had given her food poisoning JUST FROM HEARING ABOUT IT.

So yeah.

She had met Howie once, almost exactly ten years ago, when she was all of two months old. It was after that five-hour lunch we'd had when he was in town; after I'd told him I was miserably depressed; that I wasn't sure about my husband or my marriage or what I wanted to do with myself anymore—I took him home to meet my baby. I remember him kneeling in front of her, the Bear's eyes getting very, very wide as she regarded him from her Fisher-Price swing thing.

"Hi!" he said, waving at her. "I'm Howie . . ."

Then he went back to LA and we fell out of touch for a minute, during which time Facebook became a thing—or a thing we actually knew about—and, out of the blue, he sent me a DM:

"You're still hot."

And for the whole day, or let's say for the next *few days* after, I felt like maybe I was. Or that someone still thought so. Someone whose opinion still mattered. I had, by then, become a writer with a first book just published; Howie had become a boyfriend with a live-in girlfriend and a string of shows just canceled. I came to LA on a book tour, and one morning he picked me up and we went to the Beverly Hills Hotel to dine at the Polo Lounge.

"Do you have a room here?" the maître d' inquired.

"Not yet," I responded. "Let's see how breakfast goes . . ."

It was a joke, of course, one that preceded a visit filled with many such jokes and the same sort of breezy repartee we'd always had. We talked about our careers, our children, how it seemed so many lifetimes ago that we were teenage drama students at NYU. But more interesting than what we *had* discussed that day in the Polo Lounge was what we had not, namely that no matter how we "presented," we were both profoundly unhappy. Though we usually shared virtually all our innermost feelings, moods, and truths, for some reason this exchange hewed to a reflexive facetiousness that betrayed none of the sadness roiling beneath our mutual surfaces. It wasn't deliberate; we couldn't admit these things to each other because we hadn't yet fully admitted them to ourselves. And had we any inkling whatsoever of the things that troubled us, naming them even vaguely would have made them too real. Though we couldn't quite see it through the thick brume of malaise, we'd hit the place in adulthood wherein who we were wasn't who we'd set out to be; the place where the vicissitudes, the surprises, the successes, the failures had made for quite the dizzying carnival ride. In the midst of our fourth decades, we were by then learning that very little goes the way you expect—some things turn out better, some things turn out worse, some things don't turn out at all, and when you feel like you're in a free fall, the best thing you can do is have faith that if you stick your arms out, come hell or high water, you'll manage to fly. Howie's career, white-hot for years, had cooled to the point that he was, for the first time ever, unemployed. I, though I was having some professional luck, was having my own hiccups with a marriage no better off than since last we'd convened—if anything, it was worse. And yet, there we were, muddling through, brave-facing it, two old pals in peak "head-high, fuck 'em all" mode.

Like most of our repasts, our Polo Lounge fandango lasted a good four to five hours, something we only noticed when our server asked if we'd be joining them for lunch as well.

"I guess that's a hint we should leave," Howie laughed.

But if there were any other hints that day, no one was picking them up.

"I'm proud of you," he'd said about my book as he was dropping me off.

"I'm proud of you too," I said to him silently, as I inhaled the first season of his new series with his biggest fan, a human I actually made. Aside from the absolute gas it was to watch such a poignantly funny show featuring women I'd long admired, there was, of course, the added thrill of seeing a close friend finally realizing his dreams. All through our binge, every time I saw Howie's name in the "created by" opening titles, I felt this tingle of delight, this *wowza*, this *I always knew you could do it, Howie.* Overjoyed though I was and as much as I loved every single thing about this event, watching his show, watching my kid delightedly watching his show, I found myself having the strange experience of being not just buoyant but wistful—even (especially?) when something made me laugh. So much of a TV show is the "voice" of its creators, and as we devoured episode after episode all through the night, I felt I could not only hear Howie, but it was as if he were right there. It was way past our bedtimes by the time the credits rolled on the finale, the Bear dancing to the theme song, vowing to rewatch the entire season all over again. And the next evening, as she embarked on that very endeavor, I tucked myself into my closet/office and wrote Howie to congratulate him on his monumental achievement.

From: Nancy Balbirer <REDACTED>
Date: May 9, 2015, at 7:50 PM
To: Howard Morris <REDACTED>
Subject: YOU

Just wanted to tell you how much I LOVE your show: it's funny, it's sad, it's original—GREAT fucking cast (LEGENDS!! OMG you are working with LEGENDS!!).

I'm so happy for you, Howie, and so, so proud of you. This is what I always knew you could do. And it's only the beginning; you are in for a real ride. And I can't wait to hear about it.

The Bear (your biggest fan) thinks it's the "Best Show She's Ever Seen" (she's even obsessed with the opening credits)!

Anyway, congratulations, Howie—it's so great and you deserve every good thing . . .

xoxo
N

The next day was Mother's Day, and the Bear had mapped out a whole slew of festivities, which included inviting me to a screening (on our sofa) of two of our most favorite gems—*All About Eve* and the appropriately themed *Mommie Dearest*. I realize that the latter in particular would not have been every mother's cup of tea; I, however, could not have been more touched. As a mom, from the get-go, I'd always been a tad less traditional than most. I'd, for instance, played Streisand so incessantly that when the Bear aged three remarked, "Barbra is the best singer in our family," I did nothing whatsoever to disabuse her of the presumed kinship. Always a fan of the classics, I carefully doled out movies and TV shows of the Rodgers and Hammerstein / *Free to Be . . . You and Me* variety alongside the popular child fare du jour. Then, when the Bear was six, her dad and I split and a few weeks after that, our beloved dog died. And, in the year that followed, I morphed from "unconventionally groovy mama" into an emotionally exhausted, depressed-as-fuck, broke-ass, single mother, sick to shit of Disney princesses and their porn-star-wannabe wardrobes and of pretending that *The Giving Tree* wasn't either a manual for abusive relationships or infantilizing adult children or both.

Yes, we still watched movie musicals, but during the Year of Living Drearily the viewing content spiraled into something that could have easily been curated by Robert Osborne. *Mahogany, Grey Gardens, The Apartment, Annie Hall*—we didn't just watch old movies, *we lived in them.* The Bear became so enthralled with *Valley of the Dolls,* she'd unleash her Helen Lawson impersonation anytime she saw someone with a cocktail: "*Brawd*-way doesn't go for BOOZE and DOPE," she'd declaim. "Now get outta my way, I gotta MAN waiting for me . . ." Once, when she hurt her leg at school, she described said ailment to the nurse as "like Jennifer North's husband, Tony, when he kept tripping on the stairs . . ."

I wasn't exactly proud of this, and when I wasn't up all night fretting over finances, I'd be sneaking the cigs I'd been hypnotized to quit, blowing smoke out the bathroom window, obsessively questioning my "parenting style."

How many Joan Crawford movies is too many Joan Crawford movies for a seven-year-old?

On a scale of one to ten, ten being the worst, how bad is it that the Bear thinks The Cat in the Hat *was written by someone named "Dr. Susan Hayward"?*

Will she ever be able to make friends her own age if she insists on doing imitations of Imitation of Life *on playdates?*

To be fair, we made occasional forays into viewing more "age-appropriate" content, but these usually ended in disaster, like the time we decided to watch the animated children's classic, *Dumbo,* about a baby circus elephant mercilessly tormented and vilified by other circus elephants for having large ears. The Bear and I only made it to the nineteen-minute mark—just after Dumbo's mother is dragged away in shackles and thrown into solitary lockdown—before having to shut it off, both of us so utterly destroyed we sat immobilized and weeping in each other's arms, unable to fathom what we had just ingested.

"PLEASE!" the Bear wailed when she finally recovered the power of speech. "PLEEEASE, Mama, PLEEEEEEASE can we watch *The Best Little Whorehouse in Texas*? I need a happy story now . . ."

Yes, it occurred to me, a person whose entire sensibility had been seemingly refracted through the lens of an old movie, that the regularly scheduled programming might be a bit mature for my little one. Because, even if I suspected that there wasn't such a thing as a "normal" childhood, I yearned for the Bear to have, at the very least, a *childhood*, instead of being raised as a stunningly erudite forty-five-year-old gay male playmate for her lonely crone of a mother. But I'm not sure, aside from having a personality transplant, I'd ever have been able to give up or even press pause on all the old movies. It had become our ritual; it was how we mourned.

Some people *sit shiva* and some people watch *Gentlemen Prefer Blondes*.

We didn't know what was ahead for us, only that we had to keep moving. Some days that meant forward, and some days we swung from side to side or in circles; some days we did our best to jump back in time to not necessarily "before" but to "anywhere but now." We made our moves, whatever they were, together, and soon with the love and bonhomie of our neighbors. And then, when we recovered and began to thrive, our old movies became a ritual for living. It was us.

And offbeat though we were, I wouldn't trade "us" for anything.

∼

After our double feature, we went down to Cafe Cluny for an early dinner of tuna burgers and fries, then hurried home as the Bear was hosting a party for me *chez nous*. In addition to inviting the neighbors, she invited her father, with whom I had not socialized since we'd separated. Oh, we'd seen each other—at Bear-centric events like her art shows, dance recitals, concerts, or parent/teacher meetings, et cetera. But we'd not been together socially or in celebration of one another in years.

"She's making him bring a cake," I'd informed Nat the week before.

"I know," he laughed, "she told us. Troy says we need to make sure he takes the first bite."

But wouldn't you know, the party was pretty great. I had my crew with me to make me feel safe, but even still, it was nice to be able to hang with Sam and have it be not weird but instead actually pleasant.

"Thanks for coming," I said, hugging him goodbye when he was on his way out, "and thanks for the cake—it was delicious."

"Sure," he said, full-on hugging me back. "This was fun."

As we stood hugging, I caught eyes with Nat, standing behind Sam, mouth agape, mouthing, *WOW*.

Sam slipped into the hallway, and Nat flew to my side.

"Fuck the haters, Gwyneth Paltrow," he said, kissing my head. "You are a class act."

Later, still aglow with benevolence after putting the Bear to bed, I decided to send my ex a note in salute of our newfound amity. Logging in, I found an email from Howie.

From: Howard Morris <REDACTED>
Date: May 10, 2015, at 10:32 PM
To: Nancy Balbirer <REDACTED>
Subject: Re: YOU

No, YOU.

You were my first and best reader. You helped me immensely in all those years when the world didn't quite believe, but you always did. Those summer nights at your apartment in the

Village . . . reading my plays . . . I always felt so good when you would read a line and you'd crack up in the middle of it. That's when I knew it was truly funny. Of course, I only wrote those plays as an excuse to kiss you. But you knew that.

It was always YOU.

I'm thrilled that you like the show. It actually means more to me than anyone.

I miss you. I wish you were here.

There's a lot of cool stuff happening to me these days; I would love to share it with you. And I was thinking—some weekend in June (the 12th) we're (the writers) going to see Candace's play in Oregon. Any interest or chance you could come? I'd get you a ticket, your own room; there's six or eight of us—writers, mostly women and gay men, truly your crowd. It's supposed to be beautiful up there and isn't your pal Peter in the play? Honestly—no pressure, it would just be great to see you and I think it would be fun. I know it's hard to get away, but I thought I'd ask. It would be nice to go on a real date with you. I mean, it's only been 32 years!

Anyway, would love to hear about all things Nancy, so when you get a minute, give me some updates!

I really miss you.
Love, H

OK—reading this email (which I did three times in the span of one minute), my heart was beating out of my chest, my entire being was vibrating, and my breathing was rapid and shallow. Amorous *rawr* or cardiac event? Who cares? This was a *chef's kiss* of communiqués. There was nothing I did not absolutely LOVE about this email. And all that aforementioned tranquility, that relief in not having heard from him, that cool little cucumber was gone, and in her place Ann-Margret as the lovesick, hormones a-poppin' teen in *Bye Bye Birdie*. BUT . . . halfway through my imaginary rendition of "(Got) a Lot of Livin' to Do," the rational part of my brain got the hook out and reeled me in. Because as hard as I loved the whole madcap idea, chaperones and all . . . what was the deal with his relationship status? I knew from Candace his recent entanglement had been at best set to "it's complicated," but for me, it was super simple: a dame = no game. So, after I wrote back and expressed as much, Howie immediately wrote back, assuring me that his relationship had ended.

"I promise I'd NEVER put you in a weird or compromising position (unless you asked!)."

OK, cool, but was it? Really?

"How are you," I asked him, *"in terms of this breakup—it just happened, yeah?"* Like, did he need a minute to process? And, how was he feeling about it all?

From: Howard Morris <REDACTED>
Date: May 11, 2015, at 1:34 PM
To: Nancy Balbirer <REDACTED>
Subject: Re: re: YOU

I'm feeling OK about the whole thing. More than OK, relieved, born again; I can breathe. But guilty.

Oy vey, so many things that were wrong with it. I was pretending (to myself mostly) for a long while and that's no good. And what once filled a need only created a bigger, more gaping need in its place. And it was a hundred percent my fault for letting it go on this long.

We went out for about a year. It was one of those things where I don't think we ever really GOT each other, but we continued to see each other until one day we stopped.

Or I stopped.

And then four months later, she called, said she needed to come over—she'd left her bike and said she needed closure and . . . I don't know what the fuck happened, I mean, I do . . .

BEING A MAN IS SO FUCKING EMBARRASSING!!

But I was so stressed with the show and on a lot of testosterone at the time and it was making me insane! (I'm off it now.) I never really agreed to starting the relationship again. I just WENT ALONG TO GET ALONG. Which is COMPLETELY MY FAULT.

This passivity shit in relationships is all wrong on so many levels and it's what got SO CRYSTALLIZED for me in THIS relationship while working on THIS show.

Because, here's the thing: Marta and I conceived *Grace and Frankie* to be a show about HOPE. It says, "Yes, you CAN start over," even when it's very late in the day, even when no one thinks you can, even when YOU don't think you can. And last year, when we were writing that arc about Grace compromising herself (again) just to be in a relationship—I thought a LOT about that. Because I was twenty-five years younger than Grace and compromising.

For TWO FUCKING YEARS, I ended up staying in a relationship, feeling completely INAUTHENTIC. I'm serious—I never once felt like I could be myself. And this is TOTALLY on me: I knew it, I felt it, BUT because I was ALSO a lot like Sol—guilty, not wanting to hurt anyone—I didn't do anything about it. Or, not enough. It wasn't until I was at the *Grace and Frankie* premiere (oh my god—I so wish I could have taken you), sitting in my seat at the screening, that I realized how much of my life I'd written into this show. AND how I wasn't quite living up to what the show was telling me, which, in a real sense, is ME telling me—I CREATED the show! I steer this ship and I steered it right into the things I was struggling with. Grace was braver than me, but not anymore. I guess what I'm saying to you is that **Jane Fonda has taught me how to be a brave man.**

And, frankly, isn't that the way it should be?

So I was FINALLY able to end this thing that should have ended a long time ago. I do think she took it OK. She screamed at me for a while, then told me I had to pay for her therapy and her Netflix for a year. Hurting someone is terrible, but how's that for a commercial for Netflix?

Anyway, I'm turning, yes, 51 next week and I want to live my life right. I want to live it with love. Real love that I can feel, taste, and touch and give back.

So yesterday, Becca and I are at a swim meet and she's of course thrilled I've broken up with Karen because she hated her, our son hated her, my friends hated her, etc.—anyway she says to me, "Oh my god, can you please just go out with Nancy Balbirer already?!"

No pressure!! Seriously!! I just thought it was funny that even my ex-wife would like to see us together! Honestly, no pressure! But do think about Oregon the weekend of June 12th. You would, of course, have your own room. And honestly, no expectations. I think it would be fun and it would just be great to see you.

Love, H

I don't know if it was the part where his ex-wife was imploring him to pull his head out of his ass and date me or his assertion that Jane Fonda had taught him how to man up, but this email had me in tears. *Yes,* I wrote, *it would be great. All of it. To see Candace's play; to see my friend*

Peter Frechette, who's starring in the play; and most of all, to see you. But just as soon as I plunk out those words, my heart begins pounding again, only this time the overarching theme is not unbridled joy but total panic, and I begin coming up with convenient outs.

I need to look into whether I can swing it logistically in terms of the Bear, I tell him as if she didn't have a dad she could stay with for two days or, barring that, one of my neighbors.

After debating myself à la: *Do I delete this / It sounds like an excuse / Well, it is / Yes, but it's also true,* I decide to leave it, then, after a slightly more probing one-sided conversation of *What the fuck's wrong with you / I'm nervous / I know but why / Because I am,* I continue the email, admitting that there is something else that gives me pause and that is that for the better part of the last year, ever since the Darth Vader debacle, I'd been isolating, as the experience had frankly soured me on the idea of dating.

Howie asks me to expand on this, and we fall back into the continuing conversation we'd been having since 1983, and I tell him things I haven't yet even fully realized myself.

From: Nancy Balbirer <REDACTED>
Date: May 13, 2015, at 12:50 PM
To: Howard Morris <REDACTED>
Subject: OK

Here's the thing (I will try to keep this short, which means, as you are well aware, BUCKLE IN):

It had been 3 years since my marriage ended, and as such, I was no longer in grief, I was in the netherworld that comes after—an impasse, a strange sort of suspended animation, arrested between the living and the dead, the possible, the impossible. I was not married but not yet divorced, not old but no longer young. And in those 3 years I'd basically been on an inadvertent hiatus from men—a "guyatus," if you will. I say *inadvertent* because it's not that I *didn't* want love in my life—I did; it's just that I was so burned out and exhausted from being in a bad marriage as well as the demoralizing process of extricating myself from the same that I wasn't in the mindset to be seeking out men or love or even sex AT ALL. It just wasn't on my radar, and to be honest, I seriously thought it might never be. I was pushing 50 (and 50 was pushing back), and I thought it entirely possible that I had arrived at the place in life wherein I was per-haps *post*-romance, like it was a parade that had passed me by. And I was OK with it, you know? I mean, please—the last thing I wanted to be was one of these women fearing her autumn years. I wanted to imagine myself growing into this fabulous, beturbaned Marisa Berenson type, living out my days between Manhattan and Marrakesh.

NOW, sidebar to all this is that a leopard doesn't change its spots, espe-cially a slutty leopard, so even on the guyatus, there were *some* . . . encoun-ters. Like, this nanosecond I had with this potter I'd known 25 years before who was in town at the Javits Center selling his wares at the gift show. He invites me over (it's 10 blocks away from my pad) just to say hey, and, you know, it's nice to see him: we have this whole *OMG-it's-so-great-to-see-you-how-did-we-get-so-old-ha-ha-you-look-great* catch-up moment. We shoot the shit about my separation, his dead marriage, my writing, his pottery, our kids, pets, blah, blah, blah. Next day (his last day of the show), he swings by after packing up his mugs and his bowls and his ceramic lemon juicers to have a cuppa before he heads back to the wife/kids/kiln in Woodstock, and after our visit, he asks me to sign a copy of my book to him, and as I'm writing the date I realize it's Dorothy Parker's 119th b-day (a national holiday in my house), so I say, "Hey—it's Dorothy Parker's 119th birthday," and he takes me in his arms and shoves his tongue down my throat, which, to be honest, I did not hate. I thought it showed both initiative and, as a tribute to Dorothy, the kind of gesture of which she'd surely approve.

Anyway, nothing—we made out for all of like two minutes, if that, after which he hops back into his hybrid Kia, and his whole way back to

Woodstock we're on the phone, discussing how "always meant to be" this was, how it's *"kismet,"* how the sex is gonna be "tantric," etc. and I'm thinking it isn't a matter of **if** we will be together, it's only a matter of **when**.

Next day over coffee, I tell my friend and neighbor Nathaniel this story. Nat's, BTW, not just my neighbor—he's my BFF, aide-de-camp, spiritual adviser, hairdresser, and, along with his partner, Troy, god-dad to the Bear. (Yes, I know, my bestie is both gay **and** a hairdresser—double whammy of cliché, but what can I say, it's the truth. I told him if I ever write about him, I have to **at the very least** change his profession and he's like, *"Fine—keep me gay but please make me a pastry chef with a full head of hair"* [Nat's bald], and I'm like, *"'Pastry chef' is not* **more** *butch than 'hairdresser'—it's a *lateral move* at best,"* and he goes, *"Fine—make me a fireman but the hot kind in the calendars with a full head of hair AND totally ripped abs . . ."*)

ANYWAY.

OK, so I tell Nat about the Potter, and in his extremely patient, calm, midwestern-dad, Robert-Young-in-*Father-Knows-Best* way, he's like, *OK, so let's play this out: You're gonna leave NYC and run away to Woodstock with a married potter and live out the rest of your life as . . . a Joni Mitchell song??!* And, of course, he was right—Nat's **always** right, which is **why** I listen to him like he's some sort of Michigan-bred Maharishi. It was exactly the Cher-in-*Moonstruck* "snap out of it!" moment I needed to, well, snap the fuck out of it, and snapped I stayed until last year, when I let Nat convince me to go on a date with Darth Vader.

Oh.

Did I say Nat's always right?

OK, well . . . let me explain:

So, to rewind a bit: Darth Vader had invited me to his office, ostensibly to discuss my interest in adapting a book he'd recently optioned for the screen. Yes, he's a big shot with all these fancy collaborators, but quite honestly my excitement about said meeting was somewhat mitigated by the fact that Darth Vader's reputation (for being cutthroat and mean with a penchant for yelling) preceded him. I mean, after one of my producer friends told me that aligning myself with someone like Darth Vader would **only** be a plus for me if I had someone I'd like to get even with, I got so flustered, I considered canceling! But then I figured, *Fuck it—a meeting's a meeting, right? I'll take it (along with a few propranolols) and just go in with zero expectations and hope it's a positive experience.* So, imagine my surprise when, after an hour in Darth Vader's capacious lair, I leave the meeting feeling not just positive but really terrific—about myself, my potential work prospects, **and** my formidable new friend.

Back-and-forth emails ensue; ideas are bandied about regarding the aforementioned adaptation and even original screenplays; at one point, Darth Vader, who's all, "You should be seeing everything," messengers over two passes for a pre-release screening of *Maleficent*.

"I await your review," booms the Darth Vader custom-embossed note-card. "Take your daughter . . ."

And I'm like, *You know something, for someone whose brooding mien suggests he's always just one perceived slight away from his next street fight, he's an OK guy, this Darth Vader!*

So, cut to a few weeks later, he shoots me an email asking if I'd care to join him for the premiere of a friend's new movie that evening. I'm busy, but thank him for thinking of me. Darth Vader responds—immediately—with a sad-face emoji and *"I promise better notice next time—what do you want to see?"*

Now, prior to this exchange, I was fairly certain of two things: one was that Darth Vader was interested in me as a collaborator, *and the other was that he was gay*. Suddenly, I was confused and unsure about his sexuality **and** about whether his interest in me was business or pleasure. *But why?* Was it the sad-face emoji?? The allusion to "next time"? And what, exactly, about "next time" and sad-face emoji said, *I'm straight and would like to bone you*??

And please understand, it's not the invite itself that gave me pause— not in the slightest. I am well versed in this Show-Biz-y land of counter-feit coziness, faux familiarity—hugs, I-love-yous, meetings in the most unorthodox of places. To wit: my former literary agent and I once sat crafting a book proposal at the Carlyle hotel whilst Elaine Stritch stood before us braying, "I Want a Long Time Daddy," **and then** taxied to a palm reader in SoHo to determine the most auspicious date to submit to publishers. And *that* felt like a totally normal business dinner. So, Darth Vader's invitation in the scheme of things? Not *that* weird! What was, for me, hard to fathom was if this summons was part and parcel of the prosaic or was it . . . something else?

I decided to pay these concerns no nevermind, which was fine, until a few days later when *another* email from Darth Vader lands in my in-box, this one inviting me to the opening of *Beautiful: The Carole King Musical* **and** presenting a brand-new conundrum: Carole's music is the soundtrack of my childhood, and as I was in the final slalom of the hellscape that is divorce, the story of how one of my all-time sheroes finds both her second act AND her most authentic self, on the other side of marital *mishegoss*, with her kids and cat in the happy, hippie Hollywood Hills felt like the **exact** thing I needed to see. I had been hearing about the show for months; one of my dearest friends was the costume designer—I was dying to see it.

Still, though, I'm unclear—is this a professional hang or is he asking me out?

"Who cares?" says Nat.

"Because this is a business relationship," I tell him.

"Look," he says, "you need to view this as an opportunity. Yes, it's a business alliance—you've been talking to this guy about projects, exploring your options as a writer, and here's an invitation to something that's (a) very in-line with your sensibilities and (b) happens to be a musical you're wanting to see. Troy and I will babysit—**what do you have to lose?**"

I'll get to that, but first . . .

Beautiful:

So, we're at the show and it's intermission. Darth Vader and I are standing at the back of the house, and as the opening-night crowd is bobbing up and down the stairs to and from the loo, he inquires, since it happens to be the first few days of 2014, about whether I had set any specific goals for the New Year. And just as I say yes and start rattling off a bunch of stuff about my various projects, he cuts me off:

"DON'T SPEAK TO ME LIKE I'M SOME WORK BUDDY," he intones. *"SPEAK TO ME LIKE I'M A MAN."*

My first thought (after *OK, BUT AREN'T YOU A [MAYBE] WORK BUDDY??*) was **Did someone just cue the** *Jaws* **theme?**

Now, you may be wondering why, after he laid that cringy (oh my god, soooo cringy!!) line on me, I didn't say something like, *I'm sorry—I thought your interest in me was professional; if I misinterpreted that, I apologize, but that was the assumption under which I was operating; this is obviously uncomfortable for both of us, so I am going to go, thank you, good night* and make a beeline for the 43rd Street entrance of the C/E train to be home before the Bear's bedtime. Well, for one thing, I was in the middle of Carole King's life story. By the end of act 1, we know she and Gerry Goffin are over, but I **really, really** wanted to see her make it safely to Laurel Canyon, and for that I had to see act 2, **AND,** for another, I was totally fucking mortified, which gave way to what can only be described as a total and utter abdication of self (which, Howie, you will be not at all surprised to find out turns into A THEME). Right there, in the Stephen Sondheim Theatre, I left my body and the part of "Me" normally played by Me was now being played by a woefully polite, endlessly accommodating ingenue serving her best "nice girl" at cotillion who doesn't want to offend the boy who keeps stomping all over her pretty party shoes.

Yes, it was cray-cray but no **more** cray-cray than the fact that I *still* went to the after-party with him, where **the most** cray thing of all happened:

So, there we are, at Cipriani, up to our tits in marble, moola, and calamari, and I think to myself, *It's all good—I'll have a Bellini, a bite, and be on my merry way, right?* So we're chatting, DV and I, to each other, to different people involved with the production—people he knows, people

I know—and we're laughing, sipping, snacking, schmoozing, and at some point, it dawns on me:

Holy Fuck.

I'm. Having. Fun.

Now, **I can't even remember** the last time I had unadulterated, grown-ass-lady FUN, but can we *please* talk about how **wildly** unprepared for it I was (or anything even remotely approximating it) as I sat during the curtain call, plotting how to tactfully extricate myself ASAP from this man and this evening?? AND, still more cray—I wasn't the only fun-having person who was loosening up and seemingly undergoing a personality revamp: Darth Vader, normally a tad buttoned-up, is now, amid his other "work buddies," completely different. He's funny, he's charming, he's engaging, he's smart, he knows EVERYBODY and everybody knows HIM, and he's introducing me like I'm the greatest find since the Rosetta Stone and then, don't ask me how, but we fall into this screwball comedy banter and now, I'm not just having fun—I'm having a fucking ball. I mean, mere moments before I was skeeved out by this guy and now, all of a sudden, it's *What's Up, Doc?* levels of chemistry and he's Ryan and I'm Barbra, and we're sashaying through the party, all snappy repartee and DV pleading with me to join him for 3 other events that same week.

And this is how it all started, my Darth Vader thing.

But how, you ask, do you get from *Beautiful* to a bedroom in Montauk and *Fifty Shades of Oy Vey*?

Well, unfortunately, the rest of this *megillah* will have to wait—I have to pick up the Bear from school now . . . !!

More soon!

XO
N

From: Howard Morris <REDACTED>
Date: May 13, 2015, at 6:50 PM
To: Nancy Balbirer <REDACTED>
Subject: YOU CANNOT LEAVE ME HANGING!!

NANCEEE!!

I MUST KNOW THE ENDING!!

How does such a thing get introduced?? How does a guy make that *leap*? How does he make *that* sort of transition? One minute you're seeing a musical about *Carole King*, and the next it's . . . handcuffs and duct tape??

How does he get from A to Q?

I must know how he gets you from the opening of *Carole King* to *The Opening of Misty Beethoven*!!!

AND that line he laid on you at *Beautiful* was, well, BEAUTIFUL and one that YOU KNOW I will be repeating to you for the rest of time!! (By the way: **YOU ARE BEAUTIFUL**, SO HOW COULD HE OR ANYONE ELSE NOT THINK THAT??)

I *MUST* know how this *Body Heat*-but-funny story ends (I mean, I DO know, but now I must know the deets!).

Love,
H

From: Nancy Balbirer <REDACTED>
Date: May 15, 2015, at 1:36 AM
To: Howard Morris <REDACTED>
Subject: Re: YOU CANNOT LEAVE ME HANGING!!

This might be the longest response to "would you like to go out with me?" in the history of dating, so please let the record show that I am still WINNING AT LIFE.

OK.

How, you ask, do you get from the opening of *Beautiful: The Carole King Musical* to *The Opening of Misty Beethoven* (your "punch-up" referencing the '70s Golden Age of Porn does not go either unnoticed **or** unappreciated— *prayer hands emoji*):

So, one night, after seeing each other for a few months, Darth Vader and I were at the Met attending a rather decadent soiree in the Temple of Dendur. And as we swanned about, noshing on bite-size Bloody Mary tomatoes with vodka gelée, Darth Vader asks if I happen to own a leather restraint harness. Thinking he's kidding, I laugh.

He's not kidding.

"Because if not," he says, "I'd like to buy you one."

And I thought this guy didn't get my taste when he bought me a seer-sucker tunic from Vineyard Vines for Valentine's Day.

ANYWAY.

So I politely demur, and thinking that would be that, I ask him if he thinks we should try or skip the miso-glazed black cod. Nope—he wouldn't let it go (and he didn't want the cod either). For the rest of the evening—as we stood on the sidelines, watching revelers dance on the custom-built black-and-white Lucite dance floor; as we traipsed down the 1200 votive-lit stairs of the Metropolitan Museum's Great Hall; on the walk to the parking garage; in his Beemer as he drove me home to Chelsea—Darth Vader continued to wax syllogistic about how my "vanilla ladylike mom-identity" might just be the perfect yin to eroticism's yang.

So now—cat's out of the bag. And though I said, "You know, this ain't my thing," thinking that would be that—*that* was **not** *that*, and soon, even in the most incongruous of spots (like the Cathedral of Saint John the Divine in the midst of his assistant's wedding ceremony!) it became **Six Degrees of Yes, My Supreme Mistress.**

Seriously—this is what he started calling me: "My Supreme Mistress."

(Remember how I always hated the name "Nancy" cuz I thought it was humdrum and old-ladyish and felt I should have something more exotic? I take it back . . .).

And this is how it went: no transition, no segue; Darth Vader would just randomly out of nowhere slip kink into the convo:

"Can you please pass the salt?"

"Yes, My Supreme Mistress."

"Hey—where am I meeting you for the Soderbergh thing again?"

"The Tribeca Screening Room, My Supreme Mistress."

And then, of course, there was the cajoling, the coaxing, the relentless prodding, trying to pull out of me what he referred to as the "libidinous tigress" caged within me, as if he were Orson Welles and I his *Citizen Kane*.

I know.

OK, so why didn't I dump this guy the minute he started in with this stuff?

The truth is, Howie, that by the time we entered the porno-*Pygmalion* phase of our story, I actually really cared about the guy. And these feelings took me by surprise, as did my attitude when he'd opine on my prudishness: he'd wonder aloud why I was so uptight, and rather than getting defensive, I'd wonder the same. And not wanting to, as the Bear would put it, "yuck his yum," I said to myself: *OK, is there anything here?* Is there anything to the idea of embracing a more multi-nuanced, nonbinary, rife-with-complexity state of mind? What if I at least *try* to imagine myself the way he sees me, because who knows, maybe it's really true that I'm hampered by a false sense of decorousness and maybe I'm due for some sort of sexual self-discovery?

The whole experience of dating Darth Vader had been such a new one for me that *I* became thus a new experience to *myself*, leading me to ruminate on that age-old koan: "If everything's up for grabs, is it possible that some of those grabs might include a vibrating glove?"

Sure, I felt like the entire five-month Darth Vader episode was an extended-play version of the Clash's "Should I Stay or Should I Go," but something about being told I was "sexually parochial" brought out my inner–Diane Sawyer and launched an intrepid investigation into the world of BDSM.

Now, when I say "investigation," do I merely mean a cursory trip down that deep, dark rabbit hole known as Nancy in Googleland? Yes. Nevertheless, it was **still** an education and I learned a lot, **especially** in my visits to chat rooms, where I found hyperlinks not just to Reddit reviews of anal hooks but to a "sex-positive, kink-friendly, non-pathologizing" community of some of the loveliest, most helpful, and respectful people I've ever had the pleasure of **not** meeting. Which, can I just say after the sanctimonious shaming I endured on those bitchy Mommy Message Boards, was a fucking panacea?? I mean, anonymously ask another mom about sleep-training or bottle-feeding and batten down the hatches to prepare for holy hell. But if you're new to ass-play and don't know where to turn for body-safe titanium dildos, or should you, you know, need to find an inflatable gag in a pinch, these folks seriously have your back (and any other body part with which you may need help), and all without any judgment whatsoever!

They also had these hilarious usernames, like "Cock-Ring Lardner" (not kidding), from whom I learned that there are actually studies which seem to indicate kink can reduce one's stress cortisol levels (!!) and that sure, props are cool, but kink *doesn't necessarily* require a ton of expensive "stuff" ("It's not like you're taking up hockey," opined "Cock-Ring"). But I must say that it was the salient words of "Fisted Sister" (!!), whose homily on communication and trust being primo (along with understanding, patience, and above all, LISTENING) that resonated most. I heard all about what Darth Vader wanted—but what about what *I* wanted? He hadn't indicated he'd heard that—he hadn't indicated he was even interested! And, as "Fisted" further pointed out, "Boo shaming you for being 'vanilla' is not the look. If this isn't for you, he needs to respect that."

"Fisted" was right. Why the shaming?? Also, yeah, I cared about him, but come on, we didn't want the same things, and quite honestly, litmus test: I had no interest in introducing him to any of my friends, let alone my kid.

So I broke up with him.

Or I tried to.

Somehow, what started out as me ending things turned into me agreeing to going to **another two openings and a film screening that same week!** This same *exact* thing had happened earlier in our entanglement when I'd tried to break things off: not only wouldn't he accept it, he somehow, through the deftness of his lizard brain, actually three-card-monte-d me into believing that no, I did not want to break up—I just wanted to see these 6 movies with him! It was dizzying—I sometimes felt like he was a cult leader and I his lone follower. I sooo relate to you on how hard it is to break things off, even when they're not right. But this time, I *did* get him to *at least* acknowledge that we were on different pages sexually and that I needed him to quit pressuring me about role-playing and "scenes" and strap-ons and the like, or I'd need to stop seeing him altogether, period, end of story.

"I understand," he said. "But I think you and I are more kindred than you think."

And, Howie, I kid you not—for the rest of the night he's texting me:

Please forgive me and let's try to move forward. Please give me another chance—I feel so connected to you; we don't even need to speak and I feel the connection . . .

Even in the flatness of radio waves transmitting binary codes I could feel his sadness. Which made **me** sad. Like, unbearably so. And later, when I began to unpack it all, I kinda felt like this was the thing—this quality of poignant haplessness—that I found most compelling of all about Darth Vader. Because, for all his bluster and as imposing a figure as he was, there was a peculiar frailty about DV, as if he wasn't quite of this realm. I'd watch him, you know, after shows, at invited dress rehearsals, after-parties, etc., holding court, chatting with friends or colleagues; fastidiousness masking a chronic melancholia (what Yeats would call "an abiding sense of tragedy, which sustained him through temporary periods of joy"), a trait that, as you know, I've always found so winning. And it made me feel oddly protective of him. Eventually, though, the very thing that drew me in began to make me feel caught, stuck, and just like you felt in your thing, guilty.

Jesus. How sorry are you that you asked me to elaborate?? Anyway, if you haven't yet nodded off or stuck needles in your eyes, stay with me and I will do my best to wrap this up:

Fittingly, I suppose, it all came to an end the same way it began—with a Broadway musical.

It was one of those windy mornings that caused Diane Lane to make such bad choices in the movie *Unfaithful*: very last minute, Darth Vader called, told me to meet him just before 3 PM at the Schoenfeld Theatre. Unlike the glamorous opening of a future Tony Award winner, our swan song would be the closing matinee of the gorgeously lush, but financially underachieving, *Bridges of Madison County*.

Never a fan of the book or the movie (sorry, Meryl!), the musical version, with its THRILLING score and performances as unapologetically extravagant as the Iowa cornfields of its setting, should have been an instant classic, and, as I sat weeping along with the rest of the packed-to-the-rafters audience that Sunday afternoon, I was desolate to be witnessing its untimely demise.

Hours after the curtain had come down, and we'd bade our farewells to the cast and creatives at the sad little closing "party" at Sardi's, I was still trying to ferret out the reasons *Bridges* hadn't been able to sustain its run when Darth Vader and I arrived at his home in Montauk. "How could something so good come to an end," I wondered aloud as Darth Vader steered me to his bedroom.

"Was it that the leads—attractive, vibrant, thirtyish—were hardly the weathered fiftysomethings whose lives had passed them by?

"Was the audience for a Broadway musical either too shallow for an exploration of such honesty and emotional complexity or too priggish to root for an extramarital affair?

"Was it that the show, though it had received four Tony nominations, had failed to garner a nod for Best Musical?"

"Who knows," Darth Vader said absently as he unfurled me from my DVF wrap dress, unhooked my bra, and slipped off my panties.

And as I continued to postulate and puzzle over the mysteries of the commercial theater box office, Darth Vader began piling shit on the bed: a dog collar, lube, a belt, Jergens Ultra Healing moisturizing lotion (???!), and several rolls of Bounty paper towels.

I'm like, "Um . . . that's a lot of stuff?"

He goes, "There's also a machete under the bed."

"A machete?"

"Not for this," he says.

NOT FOR THIS??

NOT FOR THIS??! As if, somehow, it would make me feel better that whateverthefuck he had in mind—which *did* include a dog collar, a belt, and, god help me, JERGENS—did **not** include the preferred weapon for a Southeast Asian *melee*?? Forget about the fact that we'd only weeks before had the convo in which I said, "Hon, I know this is *you*, but it ain't *me*." Because *forgetting* seemed to be a thing everyone in that bedroom was doing, and I am absolutely including myself BECAUSE WTF WAS I DOING IN HIS BEDROOM AT ALL AT THIS POINT?? I wish I had an answer for that, Howie, but the best I can come up with is that some higher plane of my subconscious understood that because the sex/kink talk had theretofore existed only in the hypothetical, it was going to necessitate the unambiguous realness of shit playing out **in real time** before I could say NO in a way that he finally heard, yes, but more importantly in a way that I could hear **myself**.

Anyway, there I was in the bedroom I had no business being in and suddenly he's got the dog collar on and he's demonstrating how to snap the belt while telling me all the awful, horrible, mean, vile things he wants me to say (and do) to him. Again, I don't know why; I cannot explain why, but for some fucking reason, I actually TRY to snap the belt like he'd demoed and, I kid you not, the fucking thing goes FLYING across the room, and next thing I know, I'm hysterically laughing and I can't fucking stop.

I mean, I was laughing so hard I was crying (which DV totally thought meant I was "crying," but I was laughing like middle of act 2 *Noises Off* laughing), and that was it. I. Was. DONE. Like so done, I wanted to get the fuck out of there right then.

I fled; got home, and after downloading the whole ordeal to a horrified, pearl-clutching Nat, we sat in the coffee shop where I crafted a dignified "Dear Darth" breakup letter that left no space for rebuttal (I wasn't about **to even attempt** to do this shit in person). Nat called it the TED Talk of breakup letters. And though that was that, the whole thing left me feeling demoralized and deeply depressed. I kept saying to myself, *After all I've learned, here I am AGAIN??*

After months spent deprogramming, trying to unravel exactly what had made me susceptible to all this, I came to the conclusion that I had, in fact, been so starved for attention and validation that the minute I became involved with a man, I missed things that I should never have missed, whether they were subtle hints or wildly obvious affronts.

I had done this genius job—for years at that point—of burying all the inconvenient longing for connection, intimacy, the yen to be bound up in another being. I wasn't even remotely thinking of these things, because how could I when they were submerged beneath my fear of menopause and dying and worrying about money and word counts and where my daughter would go to high school in 6 years. In other words, **I was lost but had no idea I'd even been missing**.

Was I retrospectively freaked out by DV's behavior? Yes. But I was even MORE disturbed by my own. Eventually, though, I slunk right back into my guyatus, but this time with even more of a vengeance, even more isolating, because I was like, *How the fuck can I feel safe with a man if I can't even feel safe with myself?*

Does any of this make any sense??

From: Howard Morris <REDACTED>
Date: May 15, 2015, at 7:02 AM
To: Nancy Balbirer <REDACTED>
Subject: YES

It TOTALLY makes sense.

Listen, I have to get to the studio, but I wanted to respond quickly, and then I'll write more later (I know I could always call, but with the time difference maybe writing is better? Plus, we get to feel like we're Victorian, which . . . is something?).

But first, it is fucking UNCANNY how parallel our lives have been!

I find it fascinating that you've been isolating. WE'RE SO ALIKE! I'm the champ isolator. AND we have BOTH recently been in these situations with extraordinarily challenging people. I mean, even just this: When I told Karen a few weeks ago that I didn't want to be in a relationship with her, that I didn't see a future, that we didn't want the same things, ANNNNNND that I did care for her but not enough to . . . *want to see a future or want what she wants*—it was brutal, as these nights go. She couldn't believe that I was "doing this to her again"—my bad, I was—and she was never going to speak to me and would hate me forever. The very next day, all was forgiven AND FORGOTTEN. She has a powerful denial mechanism that's something to behold. It's like, if you're not fighting it every single second, you get overtaken by it. Not overtaken as much as fatigued!

But forgetting about her for a sec, forgetting about Darth Vader: there was a reason you and I needed to go through this shit. There was a reason, in terms of our growth as humans, that we needed to confront the obstacles these situations presented. And when you said you needed "the unambiguous realness of shit playing out in real time" before you could finally get out—this is so fucking TRUE. And I would only add that sometimes being in a bad thing, a thing with the wrong person, keeps you SAFE. Because love is risky, and when you're in something that's wrong, it's limited and a part of you knows it. You'll never experience loss in that situation the way you would if it was true love.

You know, the other day, I was thinking about us when we were younger. You were so open, so free, and I think it terrified me (I know it did) because I was sooooo closed off. So trapped in my mind, in my parents' ideology, my closed-off Newton, Mass., way of thinking.

And I started thinking about the play *Doubt*, which was about the value of, yes, doubt, and the idea that it's only when you doubt that you really think critically, and that often leads to change. That play was an answer to the Bush-era notion that "certainty" was all. Strength meant an uncompromising fealty to even a TERRIBLE IDEA. Doubt was "a bad thing." THINKING, EVOLVING, CHANGING WAS A BAD THING.

But what I know now is it's the only way to live. To change. To open your heart and mind.

When I was younger, I could never have imagined being a person who got a divorce. It was unthinkable. It seemed like the worst thing in the world that could happen to a person, or one of them. And then it happened to me, and I came to the conclusion that divorce might not be so terrible!

For one thing, you never have to go hiking or watch *Mad Men* again. OK, that was *MY* divorce, but seriously there are a lot of positives to the negative and they're usually not about what you leave *but what you find*. Strength you didn't know you had, skills you didn't know you had. I'd never have been the father I am had Becca and I stayed together.

Not that it's easy. But no one escapes the struggle that is being a person.

Anyway, I loved your email and will write you more later!

Love (and you know I mean it),

H

"It's seriously the most exhilarating back-and-forth I've had in, well, *ever*, quite frankly," I was telling Bibi Carrasquillo as we sat at Jenna's dining table drinking a crisp Vermentino.

"I'm dying over this story," Bibi said, replenishing my glass. "It's like that play *Love Letters*—"

"Ohhhh!" Jenna cried out from the kitchen. "I love *Love Letters*!"

"Right?" Bibi said. "I saw it, like, twenty years ago with Liza Minnelli and Desi Arnaz Jr.—"

"Seriously?" I laughed.

"I remember that!" Jenna chimed.

"Yup," Bibi said, clinking my glass. "In Miami—they were adorable."

With a flourish, Jenna emerged from the kitchen with dinner: an astonishing pasta with pesto made from ramps, those wild green onions that pop out of the ground in early springtime, setting off mass hysteria in farmers' markets across the City, before disappearing into the ether at the first hint of summer. Jenna's ramp pesto, which she served over an al dente farfalle, was, in a word, crack, and not a thing any sentient being, given the choice, would dare miss, which is exactly why Bibi and

I were there for dinner. Well, there was the ramp pesto and, of course, the sudden ramp-*up* of my amatory activity, which needed dissecting.

"I mean, OK, the prospect of going on a forty-eight-hour, cross-country jaunt seems crazy—"

"And romantic," Jenna said.

"And crazy romantic," Bibi added.

"But maybe more crazy than anything else, which is why I can't say yes."

"Why?" Jenna asked.

"I'm wanting to know this too," Bibi said, sprinkling grated Parmesan over all our plates. "Why?"

"I mean," Jenna began, "wouldn't you want to at least TRY getting together when you're both single—"

"To see what happens . . . ," Bibi offered.

"Because you've never played that out, right? You both being available—"

"At the same time—" Bibi cut in.

"Well," I said, as Jenna opened another bottle of Vermentino, "there was that time at the Sherry . . ."

"The what?"

"Do we need more wine?" Jenna asked.

"Yes," Bibi said.

And then, as Jenna and Bibi sat rapt, I recounted yet another piece of "Nowie's" tortured history: the story of the Sherry-Netherland hotel.

Six weeks after my husband and I officially separated, Howie, also newly single, was in town for a wedding.

After concurring that ours was a bone dance long overdue, we met up at the Sherry, where he was staying, ostensibly to get it on.

He tells me he loves me. I respond in kind.

We do not get it on. Shaken by the aforementioned separation as well as the recent death of my dog, I was like a seahorse fossil—numb, frozen in time, and of no use to anyone aside from an eccentric curio collector.

Howie goes home.

The "I love you" notwithstanding, a few months later, Howie posts pictures on Facebook in which he and his ex-girlfriend are at the Super Bowl. I can only assume this means they are back together. This is the same ex-girlfriend who, after hacking into Howie's email and reading our communiqués regarding the aforementioned rendezvous, subsequently reaches out to me. "As a girl's girl," she says, she feels the need to warn me that Howie's intentions toward me had been less than gallant:

I confronted him, she wrote, *and he admitted that he was doing that guy thing of keeping his options open . . .*

I'd wanted to dismiss this exhortation as the ramblings of a bitter ex, but frankly how could I—it's not like it didn't track: How many times in our history had I been there to pick up the pieces? How often was I waiting in the wings, availing myself, always ready to cuddle, to snog, to soothe? How often had I been that "option" he could keep open, or not, depending on his whim?

"So many times, I have been, well, or at least I have felt like, the consolation prize—"

"Oh my gawd!" Bibi shouted, her mouth full of pesto pasta.

"You know what I mean?"

"Of course!" Bibi said.

"I don't think there's a woman alive who hasn't felt this way," Jenna said.

"Right?" Bibi asked, rhetorically.

"And I dunno," I said, "when I saw those Facebook posts, I was like, *OK. He didn't mean it; it was just . . .* I dunno, *a moment.* And now I'm like, *Is he really done with **this** chick, or is it just another . . . you know . . .*"

"You're understandably a little skittish," Jenna said.

"I also quite honestly have been really enjoying my life," I said. "I mean, for the first time in forfuckingever I'm OK, you know?"

"Thank you!" Bibi said.

"And then I think about *Do I wanna be managing someone else's happiness again?* Cuz when you do the 'female math' of it all—"

"Yes," Jenna said. "The *Is it all worth it?*"

"The female math," Bibi laughed. "Where the numbers don't always add up."

"I dunno," I sighed. "Maybe I'm just a little gun-shy because of—"

"The director?" Jenna asked.

"The divorce?" Bibi asked.

"Yes. Both. I mean, all of it. I'm talking about a sweeping, panoramic view of my romantic résumé. It's like, maybe I'm just not cut out for this. Maybe I'm just constitutionally incapable of being in a thing."

"I hear you . . . ," Jenna said.

"They say there's a lid for every pot," Bibi said.

"Speaking of," I said. "Do you know that for my wedding, Howie was the only person who bought me any of the copper cookware I'd registered for—a copper pot that I used practically every day of a marriage that lasted twelve years to another guy?"

"The one you keep on your stove?" Jenna asked.

"Exactly," I said. "And even though not a day went by that I used that copper pot and didn't silently thank Howie because I loved it so much—and it wasn't because copper cookware conducts heat really, really well—I never bothered to question myself about that either."

"I love that he was at your wedding," Bibi said.

"Not only that," I said, "but a few months ago, when I went to cut out, you know, just a few pics from my wedding album before handing it over to Sam to do the same before we tossed it, what do I see? A giant solo picture of Howie—on his own fucking page!"

"On his own page?!" Jenna asked.

"Yup!"

"In your wedding album?" Bibi asked.

"Yup!"

There was a pause before we all started laughing.

"You're killin' me with this story, Nance," Bibi said.

"Tell him the truth about your concerns," Jenna said.

"Agree," Bibi said. "Just be honest."

We sat for a few moments just enjoying the wine and that exquisite ramp pesto.

"I dunno," Jenna said. "I'm still excited by this story."

"Me too," Bibi said.

"Also, I wanna see if you can break the curse," Jenna said.

"Oh, you and your curse," Bibi said. "Gimme a friggin' break— and, while you're at it, gimme the friggin' Parm . . ."

~

As I lay in bed that night, I thought about how, after the Sherry, I'd taken heed of Howie's ex-girlfriend's assertion—to the point of briefly wondering if the real purpose of the hotel assignation had been to arouse another woman's proprietorial feelings. But why? Because the truth was, I knew that Howie's feelings for me were never quite so simple. In all my vacillating, my dithering, my "yeah buts" about Oregon—was I still trying to protect myself or my heart? Or was it that I wasn't ready to give up the life I had fought so hard for? I glanced out the window across the courtyard at the turrets crowning the tops of the building. Even in total darkness, illuminated only by the faintest glimmer of moon, they were completely visible, which made me believe on even my most challenging days that I was safe in my kooky castle and that whatever it was that needed figuring out would one day be figured out. Emboldened by the view from my aerie and my tête-à-tête with Jenna and Bibi (*"Tell him the truth!" "Just be honest!"*), I decided to pull my laptop into bed and write Howie.

From: Nancy Balbirer <REDACTED>
Date: May 15, 2015, at 11:56 PM
To: Howard Morris <REDACTED>
Subject: Re: YES

Interesting.

That's crazy—we really are living parallel lives.

Anyway, I wanna hear more.

But, can I ask you something—do you think you're reaching out to me now cuz you just ended a thing and now you want to fill the void? I don't mean this in a bitchy way AT ALL; I'm just wondering, you know, about the psychology. Because it is *also* part of our story, the "timing issues" and how we have, for (cough) 32 YEARS, not been able to GET TOGETHER. And it's not because we haven't wanted to (aside from when we didn't because we were in things that were working). What have we been doing? How would you describe this, our, thing? Are we two ships that pass in the night, or are we saving the best for last? We are definitely a Barry Manilow song, but the question is, **which one?**

"Tryin' to Get the Feeling Again"?

"Even Now"?

"Somewhere in the Night"?

"Somewhere Down the Road"?

"I Made It Through the Rain"?

"Weekend in New England"?

"Looks Like We Made It"?

"Mandy"?

I guess I'm scared, Howie. I've had a thing for you for so long. And somehow, it's never fucking happened. Is it because we live 3,000 miles apart? I am soooooooo scared of love. And I love you and always have. But . . . it scares me. And yet, I don't want to live my life afraid, but, at the same time, I have to honor it and be honest with myself about how hurt I have been in my romantic life (even by you and I never even got to be your girlfriend!!!) and how freaked out I am about it now. In some ways, I have gotten stronger about those things, and in some ways, I am even more deeply affected. But I always, always think about you, Howie. And I seriously wonder, in the words of Barry, "if I hold you for the sake of all those times love made us lose our minds, could I ever let you go?"

I don't think I could.

But . . . I wanna see you. I'd love to come to Oregon, but I have to figure out if/how I can. If it's doable, you know?

Anyway, I miss you. It's almost your birthday. And I'm wishing you a very happy one. It's so crazy—I remember celebrating your 22nd during *Almost Romance*. I also remember celebrating my 25th and your 31st and my 35th. Isn't that funny? I know, so random. But it's cool we've been there for each other, so many times, through so many things. Anyway, on your day, please be proud of yourself for how much you have achieved in all aspects of your life. OK?

BTW: Boo Boo Bear is **desperate** to have you over to our apartment for spaghetti and meatballs (not sure why that meal specifically). She came out with it yesterday, really apropos of nothing. I asked her why and she goes:

"I wanna know what happens in season 2 of *Grace and Frankie!*"

Well!

Kid's got her priorities.

'K, babe—write me back . . .

xoxo

N

All right, I thought to myself. *This is me, unveiled and unvarnished, serving my best advanced placement adulting.* Banter and kicks aside, it was time to get real about what I needed to hear before I could even consider stepping foot on that plane. I lined the cursor up, closed my eyes, took a deep yoga breath, and hit "Send."

~

It was a Saturday and I was at Dante, supposedly reviewing a play, though what I was really doing was reviewing my last email to Howie. I had been trying to put the whole thing out of my mind, but this was easier said than done—*especially* since the Bear was, by then, on her third fucking viewing of season one of *Grace and Frankie*. And just when I was finally settling in to work, a new email slid across the upper-right corner of my computer screen.

From: Howard Morris <REDACTED>
Date: May 16, 2015, at 12:55 PM
To: Nancy Balbirer <REDACTED>
Subject: First of all

If you come to Oregon, I will write on a little piece of paper and slip it into a secret pocket in your luggage what happens when Sol opens the door to face Robert after having slept with Frankie. Then when you get home, you and Boo Boo will search your luggage, and when you find the contents of the secret pocket you two will be the ONLY AMERICANS (other than Jane Fonda and Lily Tomlin) who will KNOW WHAT HAPPENS IN SEASON 2! (I wrote the outline last weekend, am writing the script this weekend, and I'll say it doesn't disappoint! Or, at least, I hope not!)

So there's that (for an incentive to come to Ashland).

It's not that I'm reaching out to fill the void (and I do get why you might feel anxious about that). The entire relationship was a void, and I was in denial. Look—you had some needs that were met by Darth Vader, the attention, the Broadway openings, the feeling of being taken care of by a powerful man, and I had others that were met by Karen—for a time. But those things weren't built to last.

Again, so many similarities with us: I had taken a year off from relationships and women, and I was isolating myself and spending too much time alone, and then I found this beautiful woman who got me out of my shell, adored me, and suddenly I was out and about every other night in what I'd always referred to as "the Other Hollywood." The one of parties and celebrities. For years, I've only been in the one where people actually work their asses off for hours at a time and go to sleep exhausted and wake up and do it again—and, truthfully, it's the only place I ever wanted to be.

And it was good for a time. But we never had much in common—and not ONE FRIEND OF MINE "got it," other than the beauty part, and then there were other hidden factors that came to light, and underneath the beautiful brassy blonde was actually a haunting reservoir of sadness and defeat that can only be conquered within oneself. My affection for her was real. But real love was never there, no matter how hard I tried.

But *you* have always been there. In my mind, in my heart, in my thoughts. The fact is, it's ALWAYS BEEN YOU.

There is zero doubt in my mind we'd be together if we lived in the same city. OR AT LEAST WE WOULD HAVE TRIED. REALLY TRIED.

Now, no one can know if a thing, weighted down with the traumas and crap of real life, can survive, but we would have at least found out! And a lot of that is about will, isn't it? But the will can only come if it's powered by a real love. But how can we not really ever *know*? What if the best **is** for last? What if we're every Barry song all put together?

And the reason why so many people in my life, INCLUDING MY EX-WIFE, have said, "Just get together with Nancy already!" is because you have always held a part of me that I could never give to anyone else. I don't want to live not knowing that there was a great love I left behind because it wasn't PRACTICAL. Because there was distance and a daughter and a son and exes and a union of two of perhaps not the sanest of writers . . . And you've explained your "two divas" theory to me, or the thing where we're both "flowers," so we need "gardeners" or some fucking thing, but has *any* of that really worked for either of us? Because I haven't found lasting love with anyone else yet.

And neither have you.

And yet, when I was married or when I had a girlfriend, and I would bump into you, or see you with another man's arms around you, it would DRIVE ME CRAZY. I never felt that way about anyone else. That's weird, right?

That being said, there's no pressure! Pressure kills everything. Remember, we're two people who've liked each other— legitimately liked each other—for thirty years. There's always that. The question that haunts me is: *Is there more?* And I'd like to find out in a non-pressured way. But opening one's heart is a terrible business, for sure. So many things can go wrong. And most of those things that can go wrong HAVE HAPPENED TO ME. But do we live in fear, or do we at least reach out into the dark with hope in our hearts to find the thing we've been searching for?

Come to Oregon.

Love, H

Welp, I said to myself, *you've still got it, Howie. You still have the ability to stop me dead in my tracks.* I thought I knew every side of him, but this was a whole nother vibe. The mood between us had shifted; the jokes were dimmed down; the tone was honest, straightforward, and bright. Candor had always been one of the hallmarks of our relationship—but not like this. I'd never been **this** direct with him; he'd never been **this** direct with me. He met me exactly where I was, going toe to toe, letting himself be more vulnerable than I'd ever heard him. Reading it, I wanted to jump through the computer into his arms and at the same time high-tail it home, dive under the covers, and not come out until the coast was clear. I felt like I had so much to say, so much I wanted to express to him, and yet, for some reason, I didn't know quite how to respond.

I thought about all the times in the past when we'd been circumspect, not saying what we were thinking for fear of it blowing up our lives. But what if we had?

What if I'd confronted him at that lunch about his comment about "being bummed" about my "going through with" getting married? What if he'd called after me when I ran to my car without looking back, that day or any other day? What if we'd had an affair? What if any of our lunches had turned into mad fucking—in a hotel, in his office, in his bungalow on the Fox lot next to "Fake New York" Street? What if I'd never married—would we have gotten together after his came to an end? What if I'd stayed in California instead of moving back to New York—would we have gotten together after our divorces, as he'd hypothesized in his email, because the vicinity would have made it too easy not to? What if any of those times at the Brittany or my apartment in the Village, instead of pushing me away before things got too sexed up, he'd have pulled me toward him and never let go—would we be together still? Or would our youthful passion have one day, long ago, burned out?

The inclination to look back on your past and wonder how and why things worked out the way they did and if you'd feel better (or worse) had life taken a few different turns is only natural. Generally, these types of fanciful "what ifs" never venture past the realm of conjecture—they're usually just ways to kill time or, depending on your current sanity level, your soul. There are times, though, when something (or someone) from the past makes a reappearance and you find yourself in the unique position of not just playing mind games with hypotheticals but instead actually giving whatever (or whomever) a second look.

I thought about the time three years before, on my birthday, when I received a call out of the blue from the man who'd broken my heart two decades earlier—a.k.a. the Jazz Musician, a.k.a. the dude I was madly in love with who made Howie forget David's Pot Belly potato balls. To my delight, the Jazz Musician, in an apparent fit of nostalgia, had been thinking about me—first because of the aforementioned born-day, and second because he was just back from a weeklong engagement in Philadelphia, the site of our first *schtup*. The call lasted for hours, followed by another one the next day and another and another, both of us chatting, giggling, thoroughly enjoying each other just as we had all those years before. And so, when the Jazz Musician expressed an interest in a "rekindling," it felt like the most natural thing in the world that we would, at long last, resuscitate our long-dead shark of a relation-ship. But it was not to be. Because the moment I actually saw the Jazz Musician after all those years, not only was I not interested in picking up where we left off, I couldn't even fathom how or why I'd ever been attracted to him in the first place. Though the plan was to have an early dinner followed by an early roll in the hay, the thought of skipping back up memory lane to have an affair with a middle-aged man who still believed he was the reincarnation of Jack Kerouac had the same effect on me as when I considered the prospect of going on auditions again after I'd pressed pause on my acting career: abject nausea. I barely made it past the appetizer before faking a sitter emergency that sent me peeling out of the joint and diving into the first open cab.

The experience of imagining a future with that which had long ago been left behind was a gift from Goddess that made me know, unequivocally, that from then on, my life could only go in one direc-tion: forward. And as such, it was immediately after the Jazz Musician experience that my postmarital life—filled with work, my wonderful child, and the deep and abiding bonds with my friends and neighbors at London Terrace Gardens—began to take shape. For the first time in my life I felt like I was home and exactly where I was supposed to be. Why would I ever want to leave these people or this place?

For years, the singular focus of any aftermath had been about the supposed "failure" I'd just endured. But the moment my ass slid off that restaurant chair and sashayed out the door, I finally got what a disservice that outlook had been to the success those failures afforded me. How fruitless it was to be endlessly burdened by what was or what could have been. "Yesterday's gone," said the great philosopher Fleetwood Mac, and good riddance! I'd not waste my precious present longing for sequels or reboots or codas or bother to question how or why that which seemed such a part of my destiny could come to such unceremonious expiry. "Everything happens for a reason," the tough shit of cliché, would in the wake of these retrospectives become "maybe some things **don't happen** for a reason—and that's OK."

Which brings me, finally, back to Howie, a person, *also*, from my past.

"I wanna see if you can break the curse," Jenna had said, and though she was referring to the one supposedly afflicting our formidable residence, my focus was on the one Howie and I had always assumed kept us apart. But was it a curse? Was it really that malevolent outside forces had conspired to keep us "just friends"—frothy, idealized conjecture that never the twain shall meet-cute? Or were we the unconscious architects of our own design? Maybe a real romance between us was just one of those things that *didn't* happen for the simple (and boring) reason that some things just don't happen, the end. Or maybe "we" never happened because for two people with such active imaginations we needed someone to exist in our psyches in a sort of preserved amber, forever safeguarding our connection, representing all the roads less traveled or

not traveled at all; the nice idea we both harbored to make us feel better during the times when life made us feel so bad.

But how can we not really ever know? he'd said. *What if the best is for last? What if we're every Barry song all put together?*

"What you don't want to be," Nat says later when I apprise him, "is Barry Manilow's plastic surgery."

We are on the bench outside our coffee place sipping iced coffee.

"I just don't want to get all the way out to Oregon only to find out there's no *there* there . . . ," I say.

I told Nat about the last time I'd seen Howie in person, that time at the Sherry-Netherland. I told him about how we'd planned to get it on—finally—even taking a trip to Duane Reade for Trojan Ultra Thin for Ultra Sensitivity condoms. I told him about the massive make-out session, smooshed up against the hotel bedroom wall that felt so exactly like it had in room 900 at the Brittany; I told him about the I-love-yous. I told him about how we ultimately didn't have sex: I was in a k-hole of grief, that nexus between feeling nothing and everything, my marriage having ended only six weeks before, so, instead, we just lay naked in each other's arms, the box of unopened Trojans beside us, before repairing to a steak house. It was one of those overwrought joints in the middle of town, beloved by tourists and corporate mansplainers, but happened to have a reputation for superb slabs of beef and, even better, an "exploding chocolate cake"—two things Howie insisted we needed to have immediately "if not sooner."

"It's good you're going back to LA," I'd told him glumly as I swirled my spoon through the exploded molten, which was no longer cake but soup on my plate.

"Why?" he'd asked.

"Because I'm completely numb and need to process what's just happened."

Howie nodded.

"I get it," he said. "Even though you're out of it, you're still in it."

"I can imagine just folding myself into your life, avoiding or at least sidestepping the pain, and I need . . . to not do that."

"I get that too."

"I love you," I said. "But I'm actually in no condition to *love* you." Howie nodded again.

"Two things can be true," he said, smiling.

"You're not mad?" I asked.

"Of course not. Now drink your cake . . ."

"To this day," I told Nat, "I don't know how it was that I was able to summon the sangfroid to say and do that which I had so often in the past been unable to say and do.

"Regardless of a historic inability to sit with myself in the space of confusion and despair, and despite the chance to put to bed the never-ending Howie saga by, you know, going to bed with Howie, I realized my first time at the rodeo-this-was-not and that no, I cannot simply fuck my way out of the mire. Even though I still loved him, was still attracted to him, still felt all the same chemistry and soul connection as I had in the past; even though we were finally both unencumbered, I was, in fact, not free. I didn't want Howie to be a rebound lay or, worse, to dive into something new without processing my shit. So we once again went our separate ways. But, you know something, this time was different from all the other times. This time the two ships forever passing in the night had paused ever so briefly on the briny, just for a drift. And even though it was fleeting, that pause made the usual full steaming ahead to distant ports no longer possible."

"You were protecting the possibility of the happy ending," Nat said.

"We were," I said. "And afterward, we continued to be very present in each other's minds, in some ways more than we'd ever been. But that time, nothing happening, not playing it out, there was an emotionally logical excuse. No one got hurt, no one's ego got wounded, and there were no hard feelings—if anything, feelings had softened and we'd melted even more into each other even as we parted ways. What happens now?"

"What do you mean?"

"What happens now that there *are* no excuses anymore? And you know something, maybe *this* is what's scaring me about this trip. I mean, aside from all the other things that scare me, maybe *this* is what's holding me up or holding me back—that I'm afraid if it doesn't work out or we find out there's no *there* there, it blows everything we ever were to each other to smithereens."

Nat and I sat in silence for a few moments, watching the panorama of Twenty-Third Street: people rushing to galleries or the High Line; other people shuffling leisurely; one or two rooted in place, fidgeting with a poop bag, stooped over their dog's excrement.

"You know," Nat said, "when I was in beauty school in Minneapolis, I knew a girl who was in love with Paris. She'd never been, but she was totally obsessed: had pictures of it all around her place, coffee-table books, took Berlitz courses till she was fluent, the whole bit. She opens a salon, which becomes the most successful in Minneapolis, so now she can not only go to Paris, she could buy her own place there, and yet, still . . . she never went."

"Never?"

"Never."

"What?"

"She said she was afraid it could never live up to her fantasy. That she'd rather keep it as a dream."

"That's crazy," I said.

Nat looked at me.

"Maybe it couldn't live up to her fantasy," he said. "Maybe it would be something better. Or maybe just something else because it would be real. You know, it's one thing to protect the possibility of a happy ending. But you don't wanna be *so* protective that you don't even have the possibility of a beginning. Know what I mean?"

I nodded. I was starting to.

"As the Dalai Lama says, 'Great love AND great achievements involve great risk.'"

Nat and I sit still for a few moments, soaking in His Holiness's wise nugget, and in the midst of this reverie, we hear, *"FUCK YOUUUUUUUU! FUCK YOU, FUCK YOU, FUCK YOUUUUUUUUUUU!"*

It was the crazy lady from the first floor screaming out her window at the people going to galleries.

"Listen," Nat said laughing, "I know you love this place, but if you don't go to Oregon, you could end up like this loony tune."

"In her defense," I said, "the gallerygoers *are* annoying."

Just then, my phone vibrated:

From: Howard Morris <REDACTED>
Date: May 19, 2015, at 9:18 AM
To: Nancy Balbirer <REDACTED>
Subject: WAS THAT

email I wrote on Saturday too much? Am I too much? I'm so Sol! I got all romantical and emotional and that was maybe too much for you? You never responded. Nothing to freak out about. No pressure to be or do anything. I promise.

Love, H

Uh-oh. It had been three days since I'd received his last email. Three days of hemming and hawing and deliberating and vacillating and being a massive pain in the ass to myself and anyone in my vague vicinity. Three days, worst of all, of nary a response to Howie's heartfelt plea. And it was his birthday.

"Today?" Nat asked.

"Yup."

"Well," Nat sighed, "the Dalai Lama *also* says there are only two days when nothing can be done—yesterday and tomorrow."

"Meaning?"

"Meaning TODAY is the day—WRITE HIM BACK!"

~

From: Nancy Balbirer <REDACTED>
Date: May 19, 2015, at 12:06 PM
To: Howard Morris <REDACTED>
Subject: Re: WAS THAT

First of all . . . HAPPY BIRTHDAY!!!!!!!!!!

You may be 51 today, but to me, you will ALWAYS be that adorable 19-year-old boy behind the Brittany desk. It's amazing to me, given how long I have known you and the fact that no matter how long it's been since we've spoken, I feel connected to you as though no time has passed and I tell you the most excruciatingly embarrassing and intimate experiences of my life.

No—you're not too much. And I appreciate how candid we can be—really. AND I'm sorry it took me a minute to get back to you. But I'm still wondering how we can meet up like this WITHOUT pressure or expectation, you know? I suppose it would be different if I was just hopping on the A train to hang for a few hours, but this requires planes and hotel rooms.

On the one hand, how could it NOT be fun? I'm almost positive it would be. But I dunno, Howie, like I told you in my novel-length email—I've been soooo remote lately. Ever since Darth Vader I have, once again, been not social except quite honestly with my neighbors. They seem to be the only people I feel comfortable being with these days. I'm not depressed (well, I'm not depressed anymore); I was, but now my hiding away, my solitude, is more bred by habit than anything else. Jesus fuck, I guess when you get right down to it, I'm just scared. Like, I'd love to see you, I WANT to see you, but I'm scared shitless too. And maybe that's just the way I have to be; maybe I have to simply go through those uncomfortable, scared feelings about all of it.

You know, earlier this year, I reread Rilke's *Letters to a Young Poet* and I was telling Nat and Troy about this part where Rilke is telling the young poet to have patience with everything that's "unsolved in your heart." He says you have to "live the question," so that one day you will, "without even noticing it, find yourself experiencing the answer." Anyway, we all decided that the goal for the year would be to not just live the question *but to revel in it*—to not presuppose what the Magic 8-Ball's message would be BEFORE turning it over. We decided 2015 would be the Year of Yes. So, of course, Nat was reminding me of our pledge this AM over coffee and this guy, Howie, who, over the past two years has become the Scarecrow to my Dorothy, Butch Cassidy to my Sundance, Louise to my Thelma, the person who not only has my ear but my back (and on most mornings, my almond milk cappuccino), unflappable, stolid, prudent, never-rash Nat says:

"JUST GO TO FUCKING OREGON!! WHAT DO YOU HAVE TO LOSE??"

And I'm like: "OMG—seriously??? Remember the last time you said that to me???" #darthvader.

Anyway, tell me this: How would this work? When would we meet in Oregon? How do you envision it, the particulars?

BTW—I think we really *could* be every Barry Manilow song ever written. Every one except "Copacabana," that is.

Wishing you a wonderful birthday, Howie. Thinking of you on your day and sending you a big b-day hug and kiss . . .

XOXO
N

From: Howard Morris <REDACTED>
Date: May 22, 2015, at 9:31 PM
To: Nancy Balbirer <REDACTED>
Subject: Thank You

Hey there, Beautiful,

I can barely see and I know you're beautiful. My corneas are bad—did I tell you about this? Two days ago, I had this surgical eye procedure, which was fucking TORTURE, to try to stabilize my failing corneas . . . it sucked. Much pain and I couldn't open my eyes and really SEE until today. So this is me these days.

Hit show, bad corneas . . . My life has never been weirder: terrible vision in my left eye, and on Tuesday night, I'm on a filmed panel at the Television Academy with Jane and Lily and Martin.

I'm sure I'll get **lots** of questions!

"Excuse me, Mr. Morris, *who the fuck are you and what do you do on the show*?"

Just don't ask my left eye because I won't see the question anyway.

Oddly, they're giving me $250 for "hair and makeup." I don't have hair and I'm not much for makeup. I don't even know who to call!

Maybe I could use it at Best Buy . . . ?

But you can't have EVERYTHING. But can I have you? Can we have each other? Could I be the answer to the question you weren't even necessarily asking? (I'll answer that. But first . . .)

My birthday was great because it was the day before the miserable procedure to stop the corneas from getting worse, and I went out with the writers (who I adore) for barbecue and for the first time in years I wasn't PRETENDING to be having fun. I was actually *having* fun. Even when I was "celebrated" by others in recent years, I was always living someone else's version of how my birthday should be. So I pretended. I'm tired of pretending. In a lot of ways . . .

This job has tested me in ways I never could imagine and I work six hundred hours a week with an intensity I've never before achieved. And it's easy to block everything and everyone out . . . for a bit. It's weird. Like today, as I'm rewriting the outline of what happens when Sol walks through that door . . . I'm INTENSE for six straight hours. And then I can't take it anymore and I look up . . . *and no one's there.* It feels extra empty in a way. Sure, Dustin is OFTEN here, but he wasn't today. But he's almost sixteen and starts driving next month. So good luck to me! Kids leave you well before college. And I fucking adore him, as I know you do your precious daughter, who I think is the cutest girl in the world (a little tintype of her mother . . . Isn't that from some musical?). But there's a, wait, isn't there more to life than working and writing and succeeding and feeding your own ambition and fathering a good kid and getting laid by a hot blonde or two? There might not be. I'm just asking. Where's my person, whom I could be their person to? And I fully understand that having a person requires BEING a person to a person.

None of this is said to make anyone, let alone you, feel sorry for me. I don't even feel sorry for me, and I'm only viewing this email through one eye! But I just feel like I have another big love left. I KNEW I had a hit show in me. Even when I was in the desert in my career on shitty shows and various other stops along the way to career irrelevance . . . (And I do LOVE that your kid seems to enjoy whatever show I happen to be working on. She's such a peach and the most adorable girl ever.) But I was in the desert career-wise and written off by more than a few, but I KNEW, just KNEW there was something more for me. I had something more to give and someone was going to dig what I had. Many more things, perhaps . . . Now, believing in yourself at fifty in show business can be delusional, but I did nonetheless.

But I feel that way about love too. There's another big one out there for you *and* for me. Why not you AND me?! Two birds with one stone!

And then there's you. Again. Always you. You have existed on the periphery of every one of my relationships for thirty years. Even my shrink of twenty-four years says, "You have to explore the Nancy thing." Last November, I almost died of a pulmonary embolism. Talk about getting some perspective. We think we have time, but we don't really know. But what I *do* know is that I can't not at least TRY with you. I can't not LET YOU KNOW that I don't want this moment to pass as all the others have . . . By the way, you're free to reject me or think I'm insane or think you're over this thirty-plus-year, truly odd odyssey. But what if it's not so odd? How odd would that be for it to be *not* odd at all and somehow right? AND I love your Rilke Year of Yes and I love Nat! Say yes!! (Wasn't that what Angie Dickinson said to Burt Bacharach when he asked her if she wanted Martini & Rossi Asti Spumanti?? And you are just as hot as Angie, and I'm hopefully not as self-absorbed as Burt!)

OK, so practically. I get it, TOTALLY, if you can't come to Oregon. If you can, if you want to, I swear there is no pressure.

Not sexual, not relationshippy—I'd get you your own room, get you a ticket, take as much stress out as possible. But I also get it, totally, if life is too difficult right now. I guess there was something that appealed to me about meeting on neutral ground. And amid the FUNNIEST and NICEST women and gay men I know, I just figured, *Oh, those are Nancy's people. She'll be comfortable here.* (As opposed to when I hang out with my coal miner friends, I don't immediately think, *Oh, Nance will love you guys and want to get emphysema with you!*)

And it doesn't have to be Oregon. I can imagine you thinking, "Dude, you want me so bad? Get on a fucking plane and come to NYC!!!" It could be that. It could be something else. If you want to explore. I'll even get it if you say, "You know, Howie, it's not for me. It's completely impractical. It could never work. And at this point in our lives we don't even know each other that well! And frankly, you're a little irritating to me."

I totally get that **and I won't stop loving you ever**. We've come too far for that. Because when all is said and done, we fucking adore each other. You are seriously one of the best friends I've ever had and I'm (at least I think I am) one of yours. But I guess what I'm saying is, I can't not at least try. With you. But I get how the sound of that could feel like pressure. And I get how scared you are. I'm scared too. But if you can hang on to anything, hang on to this: I will always be your friend. You know that. I promise you.

Wow, I really am too much. Tell me what you're thinking. If you want to go for Oregon, tell me and I'll make the arrangements. (You'd have to fly into LA first—apparently there are no direct flights to Butt-Fuck Nowhere.) If not, tell me if there's anything you WOULD like to do. Or not.

Once I committed to going, I was excited too—very much so. Then in a hot second came the actual day: on Friday, June 12, I woke up at the crack, made the Bear breakfast, took her to school, came home, and packed. As it happened, Nat and Troy were out of town for the weekend, celebrating their birthdays, so Bibi, also a hairstylist, offered to give me a pre-trip blowout. But before Bibi's, there was just one more thing: I had to stop in on my eighty-six-year-old down-the-hall neighbor, Rosalie. The Bear and I frequently kept her food in our refrigerator—whether it was leftover Chinese from Grand Sichuan on the corner or groceries from Gristedes on the *opposite* corner or the "Italian cookies that help with constipation" from Chelsea Market—we were the keepers of her sustenance, the protectors of her provisions. Rosalie's combo of dementia and addiction to amphetamines made her believe that she was the target of a plot by our super to murder her, convert her rent-controlled unit into market rate for a new tenant, and then pocket all the dough. The super, according to Rosalie, using his master key, would slip into her apartment in the dead of night to poison the food in her fridge. Occasionally, in his stead, he'd send his henchman, a dwarf so small, he was able to crawl through a tiny hole behind the sink or somehow through her living room armoire. Since I'd be gone until Monday morning, I needed to bring Ro her food. She greeted me at the door, glassy-eyed and confused but bubbling over with excitement. I had some time to kill before Bibi's, so after stocking her food in the fridge, we sat together on her sofa.

"You're gonna miss the engagement party Susie's making for Liz," she told me. "I'm so happy for her, getting married, finally, at her age and after such *tsuris*! Lissen—it ain't easy and boy-oh-boy, Lizzy did EVERYTHING—she put herself out there: she did the Latin-dancing singles' night at SOB; she signed up for the personals and, you can't imagine (or maybe you can), it was one *farshtunkene* after the next. One day she says to me, 'Rosalie, I've gotta move! I've gotta get out of here if I'm ever gonna find a guy—there's a curse on the building!' I said to her, 'Honey, please, there's no such thing; come on, stop—this is what they call stinkin' thinkin'!' Being a victim! People are always playing the victim, why? Cuz then they don't have to look at their own shit. Look, I'm not saying life's always fair, that things don't happen to us—terrible things, calamities, things perpetrated against us that are absolutely not our fault. Unloving parents, bullying peers, tragedies, 9/11, Superstorm Sandy, the Holocaust, what have you. But buying into a curse about your love life or this *farkakte* building? It's saying, *I have no control, no responsibility for my own happiness!* I said, 'You've heard of the power of positive thinking? Oprah talks about it all the time. Well, guess what—there's the power of negative thinking too!' So Liz stops with the craziness and I'd like to think I had a little something to do with it. Anyway, now she's getting married to Ron—some guy she knew many years ago in college. I'm sorry you're gonna miss the party, honey. Let's hope Susie cleans!"

I was blown away. Though I could tell Rosalie was as high as a kite, it was the most lucid she'd been in years, and because of it, the most lucid *I'd* been in weeks.

"Wow, Ro," I said as she walked me to the door.

"Wow what?" she asked. "What's 'wow'?"

"I don't know," I said. "I guess I would have thought maybe you'd be someone who'd get into the whole London Terrace curse thing."

"Oh, please," she said, waving me off. "Who has time for such nonsense. Lissen, I got enough problems with the dwarf . . ."

~

I don't know if it was leaving the Bear for a non-work-related joyride, that my Rock of Gibraltar Nat had gone AWOL, or the fact that I was about to take not one but two flights to the middle of nowhere to see a three-and-a-half-hour play, but with no warning at all, in the middle of Bibi's blowout, I began to hyperventilate. Equanimity drained from my person, and in its place roiled an inexplicable brouhaha of dread and preperformance-like jitters. The good news is I was in the perfect place to disassemble: Bibi, shaped by her fierce but loving Nuyorican family, two bruising divorces, and a recently completed six-month "personal accountability course," was capable of wielding the perfect giving-no-fucks-but-at-the-same-time-giving-all-the-fucks-in-the-world platitudes as deftly as she did a hot iron. After bleating my intention to bow out of the trip, saying I can make it about the Bear or that I don't feel comfortable—something, Bibi shakes her head.

"And then what?" she asks as she begins to *zhuzh* "just the ends" of my already-dried sections of hair. "You're gonna spend your whole friggin' life hidden away? Like a nun? Like Jenna's beautiful painting no one gets to see cuz it's pushed to the back of the closet? When are we gonna do the things **we say** we're gonna do **if not now**? And hey—if we don't really wanna do those things—**that's fine**. But if we do, what's stoppin' us? Cuz, like, if it's just 'I'm scared,' well, yeah, OK—**we're all scared**. You walk down the street, you get on the subway, you deal with whatever shit you deal with, like, every fuckin' day. It's *cawled* life. And what kinda life is it if you live it afraid? Everyone's always (OK, bend over—I'm gonna give you just a tidge of spray), like . . . (OK, flip back up) . . . We all look at the cost of taking a chance, but HELLO, how 'bout the cost of NOT taking it?"

"I don't know what's the matter with me," I say.

"I do—you're human. Listen, I get it—it's fuckin' hard to put yourself out there," Bibi says. "But, Nance, what's the story of this trip?"

"The story?"

"Yeah, like, what're you tellin' yourself about it; how have you set it up in your mind?"

"That I have no expectations . . ."

She nods.

"See, this is the problem. *Be-cawze* expectations are *naw*-mal and human," she says. "What if you actually give yourself *some* expectations?"

"OK—"

"But I mean for *yourself.* Like—forget about him: Can you make a plan for *what you expect of yourself?*"

"Well," I say, "I'm not going to sleep with him."

"Good. Perfect," she laughs. "I love it. Can you stick to that?"

"You saying I'm a ho?"

"No!"

"Even hoes need some boundaries."

"Yes, they do," she says, hugging me tight. "You're going on a two-day adventure to see one of your very best friends."

"In Oregon," I laugh.

"Of all friggin' places—"

"What if it's terrible?"

"What if it's not?" Bibi asks. "Which are you more afraid of?"

"Nat asked me the same thing."

"Hairdressers," Bibi laughs. "Better shrinks than your shrink."

"On the way to school today, the Bear goes, 'How come on award shows they always thank their lawyer—they should be thanking their hair and makeup person cuz do you think they could look like that from having a lawyer?'"

At this we both crack up.

"That kid," she says, pulling me into a firm embrace. "She is so boss . . ."

We stood for a second, hugging, Bibi rubbing my back.

"It'll be fun, right?"

"I know it will—"

"So why am I so scared?"

Bibi shrugs, still hugging me tight.

"Two things can be true," she says. "There's no magic to this, Nance. Sometimes we just gotta do things cuz we said we were gonna."

"You're the best," I say as she walks me to the door.

"You are," she says.

"See you Monday?" I ask.

Bibi smiles.

"Go get 'em, gorgeous."

PART THREE

Ashland

June 12–14, 2015

From: Candace Kahn <REDACTED>
Date: June 12, 2015, at 9:39 AM
To: Nancy B; Howard M; Bobby F; Doug S; Liza K; Maeve M; Ted J;
Kenny P; Seth J
Subject: Ashland!

Everyone getting ready for their exciting weekend in Ashland, Oregon? ☺
I know I AM! I just thought I'd send out a group email with some info that might be useful. Call or email me if you have any questions or concerns (except Bobby—he's on his own). For those of you who are new to the group, my dear friend Seth Jones will be joining our G&F crew as well as the lovely Nancy Balbirer, who is jetting all the way from New York City! Nancy will fly into LA this afternoon, cool her heels over at Howard's for a few hours, then join the G&F writers on our flight up to Oregon this eve. Bobby's hubby, Doug, will also be flying in from New York and driving down from Portland to meet us as well, and Ted's hubby, Kenny, will also be joining. We can hang together as much (or as little) as we want, the only thing super-planned schedule-wise is Saturday eve: dinner at Larks at 5:30, after which we can stroll over to the theater for the show (I have all our tix). I am so grateful to all of you for making the schlep—you have no idea how much this means to you. Keep your expectations low and you should have a pretty fun weekend!

See you soon!

XX
Candace

Getting airborne, hooking up to the Sky-Fi, and laughing at Candace's *you have no idea how much this means TO YOU* Freudian typo helps calm my still-frayed nerves, as does the complimentary mimosa I debate having at first but then say *fuck it.* A virgin of Virgin America, I am won over by the preflight safety routine, a bangin' High School Musical-esque video that not only exhorts passengers to buckle your damn seat belts but to "live it on up in the sky."

Flight fiesta aside, in the absence of benzos, the cocktail has practical purposes: Bibi's counsel had successfully navigated my agita, but then there was the matter of successfully navigating New-York-City-summer-Friday-Hamptons traffic to make my flight out of JFK. Only when it looked like I might not make it in time, thinking, as I sat crawling out of my skin in the back of the taxi, that I had deliberately sabotaged myself, did certitude replace ambivalence. "I CANNOT MISS THIS FLIGHT," I insisted loudly and often and, somehow, miracle of miracles, I did not.

The cabin, aglow in hues of lilac and plum, further enhances the loosening effects of my quaffed mimosa, and after reading Candace's email, I read one from my agent letting me know we have interest in my book, which sounds promising, and then I read an email from Howie, which sounds equally so.

From: Howard Morris <REDACTED>
Date: June 12, 2015, at 12:01 PM
To: Nancy Balbirer <REDACTED>
Subject: Hey There

I just want you to know that Derek, my British man Friday, whom you will love, is already revving up his engines to meet you when you land, AND that I'm totally psyched to see you and hang out with you, first in LA and then in a small town on the coast of Oregon that I just found out isn't even on the coast of Oregon but actually sixteen miles north of the California border! I'm so geographic! This place is not even in the middle of butt-fuck nowhere but still manages to be hard to reach! Jesus. It's never easy with us. But remember: no stress, no expectations, just hanging.

It's fucking Oregon—you get arrested if you're stressed!
See you soon—have a safe flight!

Love, H

Could I have ever imagined on Friday, April 18, 1986, as we were stepping onstage in NYU's Black Box Theatre to perform *Almost Romance* that 1,521 Fridays later I'd be winging my way to LA before flying to not-even-the-coast-of-Oregon to have a first date with Howie chaperoned by eight people? No, I could not. But then again, I think, reclining my seat, encircled in purple, I couldn't have imagined most things that transpired in *Almost Romance*'s wake—especially the first two seminal events, one good, one bad. Well, both bad, but one a tad less bad:

Number one: On the heels of Howie's enumerating the reasons I could not assume the role of his real-life girlfriend came the news I would not be resuming my role as his fictional one either. It's one of those boring show business tales as old as the hills, but in this instance the relative youth and innocence of the players made it one of those crushing blows that can almost define one's experience in toto. The director-friend I'd invited, who'd swooped in to facilitate an off-Broadway transfer of the show, insisted that in this incarnation Howie would no longer play himself; instead, he would wear the singular hat of playwright and "he" would be played by a guy who'd just been in a movie about a robot who runs away with Ally Sheedy.

As for me, I went in for the audition my director had said would be "just a formality for the producer," and was crestfallen when what I'd thought would be my very first professional job turned out to be my very first professional "courtesy read" (a.k.a. "let's waste everyone's time by pretending to consider an actor we are in no way considering"). And then they hired the actress from the movie *Supergirl*.

"It wasn't anywhere near as good as when you guys did it," Paola told me after. "Wasn't that director a friend of yours? Didn't you invite her in the first place?"

"Yeah, but I couldn't compete with Supergirl," I said.

"You shouldn't have had to—you were adorable!" Paola cried. "She's a bad director and she's an even worse friend!"

Paola was right.

Perhaps a cannier person would have seen it coming, easily surmising that the director, whose breathless accounts of doing Ecstasy in college with a scion of the Kennedy clan, was straight-up Machiavellian from the get-go, the sort of flagrant opportunist who would milk this association no matter its relevance (or lack thereof), inserting it (sans the Molly popping) into her bio for the rest of time. While our friendship didn't survive this blow, when the director moved to Hollywood, Howie, whose writing career had been catapulted by the off-Broadway production, stayed in touch with her for a minute, that is until their association came to an equally inglorious demise: After her Hollywood "helming" aspirations fizzled, the director joined a Hasidic sect in the Pico-Robertson neighborhood of Los Angeles and became embroiled in a grifting scandal. She may have found God, but she never lost her chutzpah, "borrowing" thousands of dollars from Howie she neither repaid nor mentioned ever again. Eventually he stopped answering her myriad emails, always asking for money and to, of course, please send her regards to the wife from whom he'd been divorced for over a decade.

The saddest part of the *Almost Romance* story was that the end nearly canceled out the pure unadulterated joy of the whole experience prior.

"Howie should have made them cast you," Paola had said.

"He said he couldn't." I shrugged.

"Were you bummed? Were you mad at him?" Paola asked. "I would've been—I'm bummed and mad for you!"

I *was* bummed. And mad. And as comfortable as I had always been speaking my truth and sharing my feelings with Howie, it took me years before I could admit this to him. Partly because I was so incredibly proud of him and excited to see him getting over to the other side, and I didn't want to sully his hard-won success with my grievances. But it was also because I was, at the time, too entrenched in the quicksand of my rote people-pleasing to summon the sort of frank real-talk required for such revelations.

It must have been terrible and dispiriting for you to be taken advantage of, to be forgone and forsaken, forgotten and left in the kicked-up dust of my bolting toward a career you helped launch only to leave you alone on the launchpad, Howie wrote when I finally confessed my mass of complicated feelings. *I get it. And I'm really, truly sorry that as a young man, who was self-centered, self-righteous, self-loathing, and suffering from that horrible Young Man Affliction of deep insecurity coupled with insufferable overcompensating cockiness—I had a disease; I just didn't focus on the right one—as that deeply flawed young man, too stupid to even try to hide those flaws, I was not worthy of your love and the undying belief in me and in us that you always had. I think you're amazing for having the decency and humanity to still be able to feel such joy for me and not Schadenfreude . . .*

Perhaps, I think now, there was something fortuitous in my inability to address the *Almost Romance* unpleasantness, as distance and time allowed for both maturity and mellowing in us both. Maybe if we'd had the conversation more immediately, the alchemy of egos, hurt feelings, and youth would have led to a dustup out of which our friendship might not have found its way.

Not being cast in the off-Broadway incarnation begot *Almost Romance* event number two: Shortly after losing the part, I was cast to play the lead in another play, this one directed by my acting teacher, who, after closing night, made a pass at me. Despite the fact that said acting teacher was a debauched ex-hippie with a penchant for pot and poon, the pass took me completely by surprise. Perhaps this was because I was a twenty-year-old college student and the acting teacher was a thirty-six-year-old man who, it so happened, was in a supposedly committed relationship with *another one of his students*, someone with whom he had shacked up after his marriage ended with a woman who had *also*, at one time, *been his student*. Dude liked to fuck his students: *so what* was the apparent collective attitude; it never seemed to occur to anyone—not his peers, not the university that employed him, not even me or the other women he seduced—that anything about an aging stoner's inability to be around young women without getting handsy was at best wildly inappropriate and at worst a criminally exploitative act of power and position. It was the mideighties, but it might as well have been the midfifties since the la-di-da fuck-all attitude still held that if your much older professor had a hard-on for you, color yourself complimented and move on.

So that's what I did—I moved on. And several years later, after I'd confronted and then ultimately forgiven the acting teacher for his violation, we buried the hatchet and resumed an alliance that carried on until the day he made a pass at me *(again)*. This time, though, instead of being shocked, I was furious. Supposedly "great pals," as he put it, who were "copacetic," as he also put it, my former-teacher-now-great-pal invited me to his country cabin for a little R&R in the aftermath of my bruising breakup with the Jazz Musician. *You will have your own bedroom,* promised my "great pal," *your own bathroom, you can relax.* Copacetic? Well, not quite. See, there was no my "own bedroom"; the cabin had but *one* room, in the center of which was the only bed (there was also, by the way, only one bathroom and it lived outside). I hadn't even put my bag down before my "great pal" started chasing me around the room like a pothead Pepé Le Pew. *How* could he be trying to bed me *(again)*, I wanted to know, when it had been made crystal clear, through my actions and words, that I was not the slightest bit inter-ested in a sexual relationship with him? His response was a breathtaking blame-boomerang in which he stated that, despite the aforementioned clarity, I still "should have known how [he] *really* felt" and that if I was not "one of those awful women," his inability to control himself was something for which I should have "been prepared" and even "looking forward to."

"YOU KNEW DAMN WELL I WAS SHOPPING FOR A WOMAN!" he roared by way of a grand finale, thereby debunking for-ever both the myth that hippies are an evolved, peace-loving folk and that women are not sundries you might get a better deal on at Costco.

No matter how perverse the circumstances surrounding these events or how outrageous they became, whenever I shared this story with other people—even other women—there was more often than not something about the *Why-would-you-believe-him/What-were-you-doing-there/What-were-you-wearing*-ish line of questioning that gave off more than a subtle whiff of victim blaming.

I would learn that the legacy of these types of transgressions is that you don't even need other people to make you feel ashamed or to shade you for your unwitting complicity; long before you find yourself on the receiving end of a spurned cad's misplaced rage, you've internalized the belief that the bad behavior of men is not their responsibility to manage, it's yours. As far back as the 1970s, when it became crystal clear that my middle school's "dress code," prohibiting girls from wearing halter tops or other "distracting" garments, was actually code for "put your tits away so the boys can think," I understood that even in the Me Decade "Me" really meant "Them."

But if I took issue with the implication of anyone's questions or suggestions for how I might avoid such unpleasantness in the future, I certainly didn't address it. I was too busy metabolizing guilt and trying to dissect all the ways this #MeToo was #MyFault. I may have fancied myself a Woman Who Ran with the Wolves, but I still needed someone (other than my shrink) to point out what an endless cesspool of fuckery this particular brand of self-reproach can be and what a pathetic, antediluvian tool my mentor was. And, as it turned out, that someone was my friend Howie. Maybe it was because he was a comedy writer that made him able to distill character to a single line, but for the rest of time, from the moment I told him about what went down, Howie would shout: **"YOU KNEW I WAS SHOPPING!"** at the top of his lungs whenever the acting teacher's name was mentioned. Actually, Howie didn't even need an excuse—sometimes he'd simply call me on the phone and when I'd pick up, he'd bellow:

"NAN-CEEE! I HOPE YOU'RE FOR SALE CUZ I'M SHOPPING!"

It was as if the most woke, billionth-wave, intersectional feminist had bargello-ed the perfect cri de coeur smack into the center of my psyche. No, it might not have been the warmest, fuzziest display of empathy, but aside from making me laugh hysterically every single time, it was the only one that got me to stop the incessant beating myself up, to stop feeling (at least in *this* instance) what a massive pain in the ass it is to live life as a woman.

I will always be your friend, he'd said. *You know that. I promise you.*

He always had, through all of it. I think of the occasional flirty emails he'd sent after the Sherry-Netherland. There likely were genuine feelings or thoughts beyond the same sort of jokey, innuendo-laden banter we'd been getting into for decades, but they were behind a scrim of such waggishness, it was undetectable. I think of how in the tenor of his recent emails, Howie is—while still funny—different, softer, more emotive.

So, which "Howie" will I get now? Which "Nancy" will I be? There were parts of our old dynamic I wanted to avoid and parts I hoped we'd revive. And as the plane rattles with turbulence over Kansas (and I text a picture of the flight map to Troy, who texts back: don't crash in Kansas—those farm ladies will be judgy even if you're dead!), I am consumed with the thought that no matter how great it had been when we were young, how could who we are now live up to the illusion we'd spent years cultivating in our minds? The one that was no longer the original Kodachrome image, but the photo of that old photo, captured on your iPhone, then photoshopped and Instagram-filtered until it's so many gauzy iterations later, it no longer even vaguely represents the original but resembles instead its try-too-hard-y ersatz cousin?

Remember, he had said, *no stress, no expectations, just hanging.*

Perhaps because this time, instead of all the sudsy sexual posturing, we'd set it up more gently, or possibly because I'd been guided by intuition instead of neurosis, but whatever it is, as we begin our descent into Los Angeles, I find my emotional temperature to not be spiking with fear but rather composed and, at the same time, excited.

When I land, I have barely a moment to say, "Hi, nice to meet you," to Howie's assistant, Derek, who is, as promised, waiting curbside to shepherd me to Howie's place, when I receive a frantic call from the Bear. *WHY,* she wants to know, am I not in our apartment? When I remind her that she's *also* not in our apartment, because she's with her dad at *his* apartment, she tells me that's not the point. "Even if I'm at Dad's, you should be home, in Chelsea, waiting for me!" she wails.

Good lord, I think to myself, *even from twenty-four hundred miles away the Bear's cockblocking is bar none.*

"Listen," I tell her, "I'm just on a short trip, seeing a friend's play. Three sleeps—one, two, three—and then it's Monday and I'm picking you up right after school and we'll stop for a cheeseburger at Cluny." It is a reassurance that thankfully works on us both. That said, as nice as Derek is and as chatty as we are, the entire way from LAX to Howie's pad in Santa Monica, the butterflies I thought I'd left in New York are now enacting a brilliant replication of a Nadia Comaneci floor exercise in my stomach.

But then, wouldn't you know, within moments of our arrival, the butterflies tumble off and who comes tumbling in but Howie. It's funny how moments like this, which in reality span maybe a few seconds, manage to elongate themselves into something resembling a multi-movement sonata.

"Hey, you," he says. "Wow, look at you—you look exactly the same . . ."

The same as when we were kids? The same as the last time I saw you? I wonder, as if seemingly by magnet, I am being pulled across the planky wooden floors into Howie's arms for a long, warm *(oh my GOD, so warm)* hug. In addition to radiating his familiar warmth, his body is, as usual, redolent of Old Spice "Swagger," the scent that I will forever associate with sea captains, tough-talking deal closers, and, of course, Howie.

"Are you hungry?" he asks. "Should I order you something? I can order you *anything*—I can also get you something at LAX, but maybe that won't be good? Or I can get you something *now* AND at LAX or . . . you know, to tide you over until we get there? But that'll be too late or not too late but lat*er*, so you just let me know where you're at, hunger-wise—or *anything-wise*—and I will take care of it immediately if not sooner!"

He is amped and funny; I am giggling and silly, and in a blink the conversation we've been having since we were teenagers has resumed. In fact, so locked are we, into our playful cross talk and raillery, I barely realize we've said goodbye to Derek until, on a tour of his place, we are suddenly standing in Howie's bedroom and *even more suddenly* the butterflies have returned for a little Simone Biles handspring-double-front-salto off-the-vault action.

For fuck's sake, chill, I think to myself, *nothing's happening; you're just perusing the pad . . .*

"It's crazy," Howie says as we stand awkwardly surveying the mission-style book cabinet adjacent to his bed, "how exactly the same you look, I mean, exactly!"

I really don't look *exactly* "the same"; I'm not even sure, given the option, that I'd want to, preferring instead to view the cracks of time I've not dermatologically *zhuzhed* as well earned.

But I get it.

And I will say this: given the fact that I'm four months shy of fifty, a fair assessment would be that I look in the vicinity of the Nancy he once knew/has known through various stages of life, which is to say, *still fierce*. But then, so does he: Gone is the middle-parted hair (well, gone is *most* of the hair) and gone, too, are the John Hinckley aviators. The Boston accent, while still in evidence, isn't as "wicked hahd," and he's traded the Serpico beard for a more au courant Clooney-esque designer stubble. And, even though I see all of that, none of it registers all that much because I guess I am also viewing him through a gauzy nostalgic lens, the one that makes someone who's meant so much *to* you and *for* you look "exactly the same."

There is one thing, however, that truly is the same—the same, at least, as the last time I saw him in person—and that is Howie's getup of a black T-shirt and jeans. And this is because, he tells me now, it is the outfit he has worn every day for the last fifteen years. That's right, the guy who lambasted me all those years ago for "wearing black all the time" now wears black all the time. I find this fascinating, first because as well as I knew him, I didn't know *this*, and second that I was so fascinated about something not all that fascinating. But I couldn't help it—Howie had a "uniform"? Really? But how—and when—did black go from bête noire to go-to?

"I had just gotten divorced and needed to change up my look," he tells me as our Uber driver begins our crawl toward the airport. "I decided that anything over thirty seconds of thinking about what to wear was a failure—"

Jesus fuck, I think to myself, *you would hate being a woman.*

"—and there was this guy, when I worked on *Belushi*, another writer, who, when I joined the room, he'd just lost a ton of weight and he looked exactly like Matt Damon, BUT THEN, over the course of the season, he gained all the weight he'd lost back (by the way—this is basically how ALL diets work in a writers' room: in the span of a series, everyone loses five thousand pounds and gains back six thousand pounds over and over; it's kind of our thing, I mean, aside from, you know, the writing of jokes). ANYWAY! So now, he's gained back all the weight he lost and then some, so now he doesn't look like Matt Damon, he looks—"

"Like he ate Matt Damon?"

"Yes!" Howie says, laughing. "Exactly! I'm sorry—I didn't realize I was sharing an Uber with Buddy Hackett!"

At this we are both laughing, along with our Uber driver, who adds that *he* always enjoyed Buddy Hackett's many appearances on *Hollywood Squares*.

But how, you ask, was the writer who looked like Matt Damon until he looked like he *ate* Matt Damon the inspo behind Howie walking into a Banana Republic one day and buying fifteen of the very same black T-shirt?

"Because," Howie says, "I noticed that they were slimming. They look good on you fat *or* thin AND best of all—"

"There's zero thought or effort in the morning?"

"EXACTLY! I feel like this is an interview, but in a good way."

"Like a Paley Talk?" I offer.

"Yes! Oh, I've always wanted one of those—it's always been a dream."

"Well," I say, "let's make your dream come true. I will conduct your Paley Talk right here, right now . . ."

We have, by this time, fallen quite naturally back into our routine. Not at all dissimilar to what we'd been doing for the last six weeks via email, in person and in real time our vibe has more verve, more snap/crackle/pop than the crispiest of Rice Krispies Treats. There is no denying our mutual affinity for people-pleasing, but then again there are no people more pleased with our antics than the person with whom we are currently seated beside in the back seat of this roomy sedan. What may seem—*or even has been*—too desperate, too exhausting, too "like me! like me!" to others is, to us, a balm. You can turn actors into writers, but the performative gene will never die. It's just how we roll, how we play, how we enjoy each other and ourselves. Not unlike musicians at a jam session, trading fours, we are back in our bubble, entre nous, Steve and Eydie, and already I'm having the best time.

~

At the airport, we meet up with the Praetorian Guard of droll humans who will be our chaperones for the weekend. First, I meet Bobby, the guy who'd read my Darth Vader email aloud, who helps us figure out the ticket kiosk. Then, when we get to the gate, I meet the others. I knew Candace, obviously, and another of the writers, a giant, genial man named Ted Johnson, whom, in a strange twist, I had actually known years before, and after hugs and how-are-yous, I meet two other writers, Maeve and Seth; Liza, a G&F associate producer; and Ted's hubby, Kenny, an especially animated animator. There is some sort of ticket kerfuffle wherein I am technically seated next to Ted and Bobby and Candace is next to Howie. The Guard, desperate to rewrite this scene on the fly, *before* we actually fly, engages in a few rounds of musical chairs à la the Keystone Cops until they have worked it out so that *I* am sitting next to Howie and *they*, seated one row behind us, can not-so-surreptitiously observe us through the space between our chairs for the duration of our very amusing two-hour flight to Medford.

We arrive in Oregon, then meet up with Bobby's husband, Doug; pick up our rent-a-car; and check in to the Lithia Springs Resort. Unbeknownst to me, there had been a slight mix-up in which the front desk had been unable to locate my room reservation. As the Guard occupies me with the freshly baked chocolate-chip cookies they'd found in the lobby, Howie is meanwhile having a panic attack only alleviated when finally the front desk finds my room.

"Jesus Christ," he tells me, handing me my room key and relating his freak-out, "I was afraid you'd think I brought you all the way to Oregon because I'M SHOPPING!"

After dumping our stuff in our rooms, we repair, along with the Guard, to the local Italian watering hole. But, by the time we get there, it's after midnight local time—past three for me—and I am fading fast. So, after a quick bite, we all decide to call it a night and head back. If I were more alert, I'd have been impressed in the moment with our sans-pressure exceedingly chaste good night kiss, but it is only something that occurs to me upon reflection in the morning. Equally impressive, in the light of day, is how happy I am to see Howie two days in a row, something I note when he picks me up to drive into town for breakfast. I remember feeling this way back in the day, when we were rehearsing *Almost Romance*, just as I remember his horrendous driving skills, which time has, unfortunately, done nothing to improve. In the span of the fifteen or so minutes it takes to get into town, Howie has only barely avoided plowing into several elderly, disabled, and one both elderly *and* disabled gentleman. No one was safe with him behind the wheel.

"It's because this is a fucking BMW!" he yells. "I can't drive a vehicle commissioned by Hitler!"

"Actually," I say, "that was the VW Bug . . ."

"Not the BMW?!"

"No."

"Really?"

"Really."

"You'd think Hitler would have demanded something fancier . . ."

"He was a simple guy," I laugh. "He didn't even have a driver's license," I add as Howie almost takes out another elderly man in a crosswalk. "Yours, on the other hand, might need to be revoked."

"SHIT! I'M SORRY! I'M SORRY!" he cries out, waving to the startled man, who glares at us, then continues to putter through the crosswalk.

"I'M SORRY!" he says to me. "I'M SUCH A GOOD DRIVER AT HOME, SERIOUSLY, IF YOU SAW ME IN MY PRIUS, YOU'D BE SO IMPRESSED!"

After a late, lazy breakfast (chaperoned by only the lady Praetorian Guards, who evidently had the wisdom to drive separately), Howie and

I take a solo stroll around town. Ashland, Oregon, six and a half square miles of hot springs, wildflowers, and Shakespeare, is the sort of tiny town that might exist in a toy theater or a snowless snow globe. Main Street is jammed with art galleries and shops selling vintage clothes and books, and there's even on-tap mead, the sparkling wine-like libation made of fermented honey, in case you feel like cosplaying your favorite *Beowulf*/Chaucer/*Game of Thrones* character.

There's also the almost-hundred-acre Lithia Park, about which we heard from the second we arrived. No, it wasn't the paved pathways or trails or the pillowy roses or even the incredible Japanese Garden people were extolling—it was . . . the duck pond.

"You have to see the ducks!"

"Have you seen the ducks?"

"You can't miss the ducks—they're ah-ma-zing!"

Everywhere we went, we heard tell of these ducks, as if they had swum out of the prodigal mind of Prokofiev himself and into the symphonic fairy tale that is modern-day Ashland. But we aren't feeling especially duck-y, so we decide to just take an after-breakfast walk.

After wandering around Main Street for a while, we happen upon an ice-cream parlor called BJ's.

"Do you think they're fucking with us?" I ask.

"They said to themselves, 'Guys—what could we name our place that would make people think of licking an ice-cream cone?'"

We don't feel like licking an ice-cream cone, but we *do* feel like getting out of the sweltering Ashland heat, so we buy two bottles of cold water and, sitting opposite each other in a pair of leather club chairs up front, we continue our faux "Paley Talk."

"See," I tell him, "I can find a way to interview you anywhere."

But Howie has other plans; he wants to interview *me* about BDSM—specifically the part wherein partners are supposed to come up with "scripts" for the various scenarios.

"So, lemme get this straight: you're the writer AND the talent?" Howie asks.

"Yes—"

"Gotcha . . ."

"And the 'scenes' can be anything you want. They can be super simple or crazy elaborate with, like, period costumes . . ."

"Period costumes?!"

"As long as you both agree to it, yeah."

"You mean like *Downton Abbey* with Ben Wa balls?!" Howie asks. "Somehow I can't picture Lady Mary in a 'bondage hood.'"

Something about this visual makes me laugh so hysterically that I begin to slide off my leather club chair, which, in turn, makes Howie laugh. Just like in the old days, *nothing* makes Howie laugh harder than when *I'm* falling on the floor, laughing at one of *his* jokes. Our laughter goes on for a few moments, families with young children merrily enjoying scoops of ice cream all around us.

"By the way," Howie asks, "were the scripts you guys came up with any good? Thrillers? Anything we could maybe pitch to Netflix?"

"It never got that far—he'd say, 'Yes, My Supreme Mistress,' and I'd be, like, actor's-nightmare-level stumped. Total blank. Nothing."

"And it's not like you could yell, 'Line!'"

"Do you remember how I used to have that recurring dream where I'm in the musical *Cats* and it's the opening number and the orchestra starts playing the first few bars and I have no idea which cat I'm playing, and I'm like, *OH MY GOD, THE SONG'S STARTING—WHICH FUCKING CAT AM I?*"

"I remember—"

"Actually, now that I think of it, there *were* other lines: every now and then, to whet my imagination, he'd say shit like, '*You're very powerful.*'"

"*Ohhhhh,*" Howie says, his eyes widening. "I LOVE that!"

"'*You have no idea how incredibly powerful you are*' . . . shit like that . . ."

"Oh my god—that is SO GREAT."

"Uh-oh."

"What?"

"Is this gonna be one of those things you repeat to me ad nauseum for the rest of time?"

"A hundred percent," he says. "You mean like 'I'M SHOPPING!'? For sure . . ."

"By the way—speaking of *Cats*: 'scenes' can be completely fantastical with no basis in reality whatsoever. Like, you'll have one person playing Regular Human and the other playing—"

"Grizabella the Glamour Cat?"

"Piece of Furniture."

"Hold it: one person is playing Regular Human—"

"Yes."

"And the other is playing Piece of Furniture?"

"Correct."

"So it's Theatre of the Absurd."

"Exactly—straight out of Genet. And then, sometimes, it can be very sort of pedestrian, like Handyman and Lonely Housewife . . ."

Howie's face lights up.

"Oh, I could do that one! But could it be Lonely Housewife and Incompetent Handyman with Easy-to-Accomplish Task?"

"That works!" I say, laughing.

"Like, nothing from IKEA . . ."

"Exactly. But I think the most important thing I learned is that if your partner's a kinkster and that's not your jam, it's most likely too big a difference to overcome . . ."

Howie nods. "It's hard enough making a relationship work without having to turn yourself into an ottoman . . ."

"Do you think maybe I needed to be with someone who reminded me of the power I'd surrendered while being in a bad relationship for so long? And, OK, the pitch for how I might reclaim said power wasn't my thing, but, in the grand scheme of things, maybe that wasn't the point?"

"No," Howie says. "I think you just needed to hit rock bottom. You had to go to an extreme, like I did in my last thing, because it puts you on the right track. The scariest thing is something in the middle, 'cause it's so easy to settle. I mean, why was I with all those wrong women in the last few years—women NO ONE thought were right for me? Was I protecting myself? Yes. But you get what you get when you don't risk anything—and you don't get much. And that's fine . . . until it isn't. It's, you know, the Barry Manilow line: 'It's all very nice, but not very good.'"

"A friend of mine, she's a kinda-Buddhist, and she's always reminding me to celebrate my mistakes and foibles."

"It's called being human—"

"'Falling off the path *is* the path.'"

"Oooh—I love that."

"That's what she's always saying."

"I'm totally using that from now on anytime I fuck things up. You think I can lay that line on our network executives if they don't like the next script?"

This makes us laugh.

"Not sure that one'll work, but I'm still using it!"

"By the way, and speaking of relationships," I say, "did you hear about Dave and Bridget?"

"Oh, no."

"Yup."

"Over?"

"Yup."

"They'd been together for what—thirtysomething years?"

"Yup."

"Jesus," Howie says, shaking his head sadly. "Does *anything* last?"

"Well, in fairness, Dave knocked up a Catholic girl when they were barely twenty years old, so . . . not exactly the ideal way to begin a marriage . . ."

"Or parenthood—"

"No," I say. "But, to answer your question, I honestly don't know. I mean, nothing's ever worked out for me."

We pause for a beat, just looking at each other, two people who've seriously been through the mill relationship-wise.

"How did I end up like this, Howie?" I ask. "How did I end up almost fifty and all alone when all I ever wanted, aside from my kid, was love? How the fuck did that happen? It's so strange, though—I'm actually really happy, like really content in a way I've never been, you know? And this is the longest I've ever been single and I'm like, *This is why—this is good for me,* you know? And then all of a sudden I'm like, *How the hell does Jess have a boyfriend?* and I wonder if I'm just kidding myself . . ."

"Who's Jess?" Howie asks.

"Jess is a friend of mine—the mom of one of the Bear's school chums—"

"And, I take it, she has a boyfriend," Howie says.

"A couple of months ago," I tell him, "Jess finally dumped her ne'er-do-well husband of fifteen years and, *the same week*, hooked up with the buff part-time trainer, twenty years her junior, she'd recently hired to be her kids' 'manny.'"

"Niiice . . ."

"I know! It *is* nice! And when I found out, I was thrilled for her. But in that same moment, this wave of fucking sadness came over me and all I could think was . . ."

"How the hell does Jess have a boyfriend?" Howie says.

"Yes!" I say, laughing. "And I don't even know *what* it was about because it's not like I was bemoaning my life or anything even remotely like that. I was fucking happy! I *am* happy! At least I thought I was."

"Listen," Howie says, "I don't think there's a person on the planet who doesn't ask themselves some version of *How the hell does Jess have a boyfriend?*—happy or not."

"I guess I don't fully understand myself," I tell him. "Most of the time, especially since my divorce was finalized, I feel fanfuckingtastic—about myself, about my life; I mean, yeah, OK, I want more money, more opportunities, stuff for my kid, blah, blah, blah, but generally speaking, I'm feeling pretty goddamn blessed about all of it. But then sometimes—not always, mind you—but every now and then I see couples on the street, out and about, like at this place," I say, looking around at the BJ's patrons, "and I'm like, *Why can't I have this?* And it's so out of nowhere, this thought, and so dismantling until I remember how terrible it feels to have it all end, and then I'm like, *You know something, I'm actually better off alone.*"

We pause for a second, looking at each other.

"But then, I wonder . . ."

"Wonder what?" Howie asks.

"If that's just the story I tell myself to get through the night."

Howie nods but says nothing. He doesn't need to. He gets it.

"One thing's for sure, though," I tell him as we get up to leave BJ's. "I am never getting married again."

A few hours later, we meet up with the Guard to dine at a divine place near the theater called Larks. It's just the sort of boîte you'd hope to find after a hot day, on the edge of the world, unmoored as you are from your normal life. Billed as "an oasis of art deco gentility nestled in the Rogue Valley," Larks's menu featured the hallmarks of the Pacific Northwest at its seasonable and sustainable, cage-free, grass-fed, locally sourced, farm-to-table-y best: grilled salmon, fried chicken, crab fritters, home-baked bread, elk (yes), and just the right amount of Gallic influence to make you feel like maybe the elk offering *wasn't* a tad too on-the-nose. When I sit down next to Howie, after the "mixologist" suggests and then brings an artisanal cocktail made of tequila, lime, agave, and muddled plums, all eyes are on me while Ted, in the nicest, most benign way, begins to casually interrogate me.

What was I up to these days; what was I working on; what's new life-wise, New York–wise?

Everyone beams at me, nods at me enthusiastically, watches beatifically as Howie and I relate.

For the first time since I'd arrived in Ashland, my stomach starts to flutter with nerves.

It hits me that this is an audition; it's like when you're an actor and someone thinks you might be perfect for a role in a project for which they have already cast their leading man. They can't just offer the part to you, but, at the same time, your status is such that they can't ask you to audition. Instead, you are invited in for something euphemistically called a "chemistry read," so everyone can make sure the vibe is right for the love interests. I look around the table at the grinning faces and it dawns on me: oh, that's right, this table of writer-producers *basically knows everything*. And it also dawns on me how invested they all are; how up in each other's business people get when they spend all their time together, barricaded in a room for hours at a time, trying to make each other laugh, telling each other the stories of their lives to mine for the stories in their scripts. It is a gig which cannot help but become on a daily basis a ginormous therapy session—unloading, advising, relating issues, and ultimately working out the same through the characters of whateverthefuck series they happen to be on. And in these rooms, the denizens cannot help but become close, in some cases closer than humans you've known for twice as long. They laugh together, they argue together, they eat together, they joy together, they grieve together. Over the course of what will be, at the end of its run, seven seasons of television, the writers of the *Grace and Frankie* room will watch each other, in no particular order, get married, get divorced, get pregnant, get cancer, find love, find brain tumors, break engagements, and die. So, by definition, the gamut.

I am not offended by this "audition"—I get it. And more than that I feel, despite my butterflies, very at home with these people. I see how they love Howie, what their friendship has done—is doing—for him. I am clearly the guest of honor at this table, but unlike the times I'd been invited into these spaces and *actually* auditioned for television producers, the Praetorian Guard is going out of their way to make sure I know how much they believe I am right for the part. As such, conversation, jokes, banter flow easily and freely. Howie is on my left, and to my right is Bobby and his husband, Doug, whom I learn is a publicist and as funny as Bobby. Giant, genial Ted is seated directly across from me; to his right is his husband, Kenny; and to his left is Candace, who tells the hilarious but sadly predictable tale of how people in Hollywood reacted to the news she had written a play.

"'Oh my god, she's aged out of television—how sad!' was the poop making its stinky way across town (of course it got back to me)," Candace laughs. "No one could imagine that I might write a play *because I wanted to*—who in their right mind would do something like that?!"

"You're definitely not aging out of our show!" Howie says.

"No," Ted says, "you are just the right amount of over the Hollywood Hill!"

"Awww—you guys are the best," Candace says. "I'm so happy you all came all this way—"

"You have no idea how much this means **to YOU**," Bobby says, raising his glass. "To Candace, mazel tov . . ."

I lean back in my chair, soaking it all in. I don't know if it's solely thanks to our plummy cocktail, so delicious we've ordered another, that I feel an intensely warm buzz in the center of my fourth chakra, radiating out until the tips of my limbs are aglow like ET's finger, but

I am exceedingly turned on. By Howie, this place, this evening, this vibe. For the first time ever in our adult lives, I am with Howie in his element, in his world, with his peeps, seeing how they love him, how he loves them; feeling what it is to be with him, not just as a friend but as a grown woman experiencing the unambiguous attention of a grown man. *I can picture myself with you*, I think, *in your life, with these people, who feel an awful lot like my people too.*

At the end of the dinner, on my way to the ladies' room, I hear Kenny screech, *"Is this a date?!"* to Howie. I hurry away so as not to hear his response.

We go to the play. It is an emotionally rich, plot-twisty thriller and a stunning achievement, but my jet lag is such that even though I'm "off caffeine," I need some during the second intermission or I know I won't be able to keep my eyes open through the third act.

"Come on," Howie says, taking my hand, "let's get you some coffee."

We haven't held hands in years—since the time he was in New York, four years before. I remember him taking my hand on the street, in front of the Sherry-Netherland, as we ran across Fifty-Fourth Street, en route to buying the condoms we never used. I remember in that moment doing the math to figure out how long it had been since he'd last reached for my hand and realizing it was twenty-one years before at David's Pot Belly. His hand is, as I remember, as warm and generous as he is. It's a feeling so familiar but, at the same time, so uncommon to me. I recall how wispy I felt, though I was the one boldly steering us toward Duane Reade, the one who was so insistent that sex was a thing we'd be having. This night, though, I am sleepy and happy to let Howie just take care of me, a thing I've not heretofore been super comfortable with, not just with Howie but with anyone. But, in this instance, I like it. And though none of this is typical, it feels completely and also refreshingly normal.

After the performance, we all head to the late-night Italian place of our first night, along with Candace and the cast, which includes my friend Peter, whose performance was marvelous.

"It's so great being together," Peter says as we huddle. "Has it really been five years?"

"Since you left New York," I say.

"Oh my god—I remember our last dinner, or was it lunch?"

"Lunch," I tell him, "at Westville."

"We knew the next year would bring different things," he says, "but we had no idea *how* different . . ."

We make a pact to not let so much time go by without seeing each other.

"I'll be out to LA to visit you," I blurt out.

Everything stops—all clinking, clanking, drinking, dranking—and it's dead silent, no one moving a muscle, like in those old "when EF Hutton talks, people listen" commercials.

"Erm, you mean, like, when you visit . . . Howie?" Peter asks, feeding me my line.

That is what I meant—exactly what I meant. I just didn't realize that I meant it. Yet.

After another chaste kiss good night, we pull apart and . . . swoop back in, only this time for a kiss that has that ever-so-slight pause before the soupçon of tongue that usually heralds the inception of massive making out. BUT, no. I can't. I cannot, nope—NO.

Because I'd promised myself a weekend sans woo, sans getting so carried away and losing myself, as I so often had, in the belief that the best part of love, as the Air Supply song goes, "is the thinnest slice"— no. I needed to check myself, to keep my wits about me and my pants on because, let's face it, historically, it took but one lay for me to be rendered too dick-mo-tized to function on my own behalf. I refuse to be undone by a kiss any more than I want to be *done in* if whatever *this* is doesn't work out. So I pull away and say simply, "Good night, Howie."

"Good night," he says, "sleep tight . . ."

And, with that, we retreat to our respective boudoirs.

I am impressed with us both for this level of restraint, I think, as, washing my face free of the evening's makeup, I stare in the mirror. I have no idea what time it is, or more accurately, what my internal time is given the late hour and the time difference, but I have now leaned into the slaphappiness of exhaustion so far that I have come full circadian circle into total insomnia. I look at the ginormous soaking tub with the fluffy robe draped over its side and the equally lush slippers just beneath, and I decide to light some candles and have a soak in some mineral-rich water. And though my body begins to float and unwind, my thoughts continue to survey and to parse.

"One thing's for sure," I had told him at BJ's, *"I am never getting married again."*

Just three months before, as we sat splitting a cheeseburger and a glass of rosé at the Red Cat bar on Tenth Avenue, Jenna had asked me, now that my divorce was at long last finalized, to name the thing that had surprised me most about marriage.

"How much I actually liked it," I told her.

The obvious surprise of this was because my ex-husband and I were miserable in our efforts to save the marriage and equally if not more miserable in our efforts to bury it. What had been lost to time was the fact that prior to meeting my ex, I was not a big believer in conjugality. I took a more bohemian view, while my ex-husband believed in marriage and its sanctity. Because I loved him, I figured, *OK—I'll do this and I'll do it once*—no biggie. When our rabbi spoke of the auspiciousness in marrying on the first night of a new moon, pointing out the "unequivocal faith one must have to venture forth in darkness," I believed with every fiber of my being that love would light the way for us, always.

"Always," it turned out, was around four years, after which the dark became so all-encompassing, we not only could no longer see our way, we could no longer see the point.

But even still, I had no regrets about hopping onto a wagon I'd theretofore found corny and old-fashioned. On the contrary, I left still feeling love for my husband and for marriage, even if neither one had worked out for me. If anything, I blamed myself for the failure, owing the same to my own brokenness. To overcompensate, I outwardly adopted an easy rote-reflexive cynicism; inwardly, however, I did my best to avoid examining how utterly destroyed I really felt.

Then one night, in the aftermath of my separation, I attended a "mom dinner" at the home of a friend. The friend, someone I'd known for years, announced, apropos of nothing, to the assembled moms seated around her dinner table, that despite having a husband, a son, a brother, and a dead dad, all of whom she loved, she hated men.

"They suck," she said, slurping the remains of her famous spaghetti and "cheater sauce," a special concoction of Trader Joe's Organic Marinara, doctored to the gills with dried herbs and way too much garlic.

It was a revelation that, while abrupt, seemed to stun no one at the table save for me, though I betrayed none of it in the moment; I simply continued picking my way around the shards of garlic, listening silently to the cacophony of voices around me yelping in agreement. It was not my friend's truth that surprised me; I knew that, though she claimed to love her husband, she in fact hated her husband, a rage-aholic-y soap actor who made the sort of obnoxiously large salary you always hear about men with little to no talent making just for having pecs and an ability to project a certain monosyllabic "intensity." I knew she hated her husband and that, furthermore, her husband hated her because it was impossible to *not* know this—their brawls, as predictable as the sun, knew no bounds and even less modesty. Individually, they were good people—kind, generous, vegan, dog rescuing. Together, though, they were the *Apocalypse Now* of relationships.

You might think, given these particulars, that years later, when they finally divorced, my friend's abhorrence of men would abate, but you would be wrong. Not only did my friend's feelings toward the male species NOT wane, they grew even more acute. But *even this* wasn't what really surprised me, nor was I surprised hearing similar pronouncements from other women in and out of unhappy marriages. What surprised me, as I sat there at that dinner table and then later in reviewing this event, was the fact that when it came to the subject of men, for the first time ever, I felt nothing. Not hate, not like—nothing. I was astonished—*how could it be*, I wondered, and *when did it happen, when had that particular corner been turned and why had it eluded my notice?*

At one point—too many points in fact—my life revolved around not just men but my feelings about men, my obsession with men: what they thought, how they felt, how they viewed me, how I might change (or not) that view. For years, their lives, their careers, their yens were always the main course and everything I was into or about was the accompaniment, the small plate, the thing you could maybe switch out for another thing or decide to not have at all if you were disinclined or dieting.

Marriage brought its own brand of codependence, but even as our mutual ardor began to fade, what my spouse said, did, or thought about what I said, did, or thought was maddeningly consequential enough to shade, if not wholly alter, whatever I said, did, or thought. It was only after it all went up in smoke that the tide of indifference, as far as men were concerned, rolled in, where it stayed until the night Darth Vader took me to the *Beautiful* opening, whereupon, it rolled back out to sea and, along with it, a stunned and rudderless me. Once I made my way out of the undertow and back to shore, I began to see that what I'd mistook for apathy at that mom dinner was, in fact, a sort of natural postmarital paralysis, which preceded an equally natural period of postmarital *overcorrection*, like when your car hits a patch of ice, and in your effort to stave off collision, you inadvertently steer yourself into a more consequential wreck (or a strap-on). A chastening experience, to be sure, but as bewildering as it was to have found myself in Darth Vader's brawny grasp, I was equally confused, in our fling's wake, by how much credence and weight I'd given to his opinion of me, how available I was to throw myself over.

I'd been in the process of recovery when he muscled his way into my life, and not just from a failed marriage, but recovery as in an actual *excavation of self*. And, to my surprise, I had for the first time ever been digging what I dug up. I was reanimated and wildly productive: more creative, more inspired, more enthused, more driven, more myself, happier, and *more free* than ever before, or at least since banging about the unbridled corridors of my youth. When into my dervish whirled Darth Vader like a moth to flame, or perhaps more aptly, a junkie to smack, I began, once again, to question and doubt myself, and that was only when I considered myself at all. Luckily, our entanglement was, in the scheme of things, relatively short and I was able to quickly course correct and get myself back on track, but the episode itself was instructive. Besides absorbing the general wisdom that one's personal growth is not linear but serpentine (and often circuitous), I learned something about myself, and that was that I still loved love. And nothing—not endless heartbreak, not being with the wrong person or even being benumbed via the waterboarding of divorce—would ever change that. It was a truth as much a part of the authentic me I'd exhumed as anything else. But it was also a truth that frightened the fuck out of me, given my atrocious track record.

I became thus resigned to not being against romance per se but to the possibility of being, as I'd described in my email to Howie, *post*-romance. In the abstract, I still longed for what I'd always longed for—connection, intimacy, "touching souls," like Joni says in "A Case of You."

I just wasn't sure I was capable of being my most authentic, hard-won self, or of achieving the kind of work-self-mothering balance to which I aspired if I added love and men to my mix. So, in the absence of definitive answers, I wound myself right back to my previous state of casual disaffection, never bothering to wonder if these feelings might be the transitory, emotional stopgap they'd been before.

"Is your fear that it doesn't work out with Howie," Nat had asked before I said yes to the trip, *"or are you more afraid that it does?"*

This is the question rolling around in my head as I transfer myself from bath to bed, where I lie swaddled in the fluffy white robe, ruminating, still punchy and unable to sleep.

That kiss.

Oh my fucking god, it was heaven.

Then why am I *still* so scared?

"Two things can be true," Bibi had said.

Just then, Cher's "Believe," which is Nat's ringtone, pierces through the Arcadian Zen.

Nothing, he texts, just thinking of you. Hope you're having fun!

I think of how we came up with this ringtone, when, on our first date with the Bear and Troy to see *Funny Face*, "Believe" came on the taxi's radio. We were all singing the chorus loudly, except that I, in an embarrassing mondegreen, thought the lyric "Do you believe in LIFE after love" was "Do you believe in LOVE after LOVE."

Nat, of course, never let me live this down and so it became his ringtone.

"I think it's Freudian," I told him at the time. *"I'm not so sure I do believe in 'love after love.'"*

"*I dunno,*" he'd said. "*I think you misheard it because you* want *to believe in love after love—so bad.*"

"I think you're right, Nat," I say now. I just want the kind that can last.

"*Does anything last?*" Howie had asked me.

Yes, I think to myself, *friendship. And love.* This is, of course, not always the case, but this is what I thought when he asked me and it's what I am suffused with now as I drift off, finally, to sleep. *Friendship* and *love . . .*

~

In the morning, when I wake, there is a message from Howie on my voice mail. He asks me if I remember the Barbara Walters special in which James Brolin claimed that his obsession with Barbra Streisand was such that he misses her when he's sleeping because, if so, he wants me to know that he feels the exact same way about me. Of course he knew that I not only remembered it, I'd memorized it. How could I not have? The one time Barbra, so famously prickly in interviews, was behaving like a giddy, giggly, lovey-dovey teen is not something any self-respecting Barbraphile could so easily forget. To recap:

A mutual friend invited Barbra and James to a dinner party with thirty other people, the ruse being we will disguise this "blind date" as a "dinner," so there's no pressure (sound familiar?).

So, on the *20/20* special, Barbara Walters asks Barbra Streisand, "Did you ever think that this would happen to you in quite this way?" and James says, "No. I know you're talking to her *(he points to Barbra, nestled in the crook of his arm/in his lap)*, but NO, not to me." And then Barbra says, "No. You just can't imagine it. But you've imagined it your whole life, but then you can't imagine it cuz it's never happened, and then it happens and then you can't imagine it, but you'd imagined it all the time, but now it's here, so it's hard to imagine." Which, to me, is the single greatest description EVER of the delicious wonder and surprise that is falling in love. I don't think Howie remembers this interview verbatim as I do (in fact, I am sure of it), but the fact that he pulls the reference out of his snood warms the cockles of my heart in such a specific secret-language way that, despite my sleep-deprived stupor, I am pogo-sticking around my room as I pack my things.

The thing about this interview, though, aside from the aforementioned genius of Barbra's madcap elucidation, is that when it aired, the Brolin/Streisand extravagant display was widely mocked, a detail Howie reminds me of when he comes to collect me.

"Why do you think that is?" I ask him as I zip my carry-on and do a final room check for unpacked items.

"People were wondering, *Is this for real or for the camera?*"

"I don't think so," I say. "I think it was a cocktail of envy and cynicism that made people make fun of them, and I say this not just as a superfan but as a cynical someone who envied them."

Howie smiles.

"That's funny," he says, taking my bag. "When I was feeling all Brolin-y this morning, I was like, *When's the last time I missed someone so much I couldn't wait for them to wake up so I could tell them something?* and I was like, *Oh, right, never . . .*"

We go back to the same place we'd brunched the morning before and find a table for two next to an elderly couple, the only other people eating inside.

As we are seated, my mind flashes on what I'd said to Peter; how my fatigue had prompted my id to act as Cyrano, presupposing foreseeable travel to Los Angeles. I flash on Howie saying *There is zero doubt in my mind we'd be together if we lived in the same city. OR AT LEAST WE WOULD HAVE TRIED* in his email.

I believe this is true—we would probably have tried and we likely would right now too—if we lived in the same place. But we don't and because of the effort "trying" would require in terms of travel and logistics, I don't want nor feel the need to mince words: I ask Howie how he thinks it might work—what he was envisioning.

"Well," he says, "I'd make sure we saw each other as much as possible—every few weeks—either I'd fly you out to see me or I'd fly in to see you. We'd make a schedule so we're both doing the traveling and just figure out how to make it happen."

His chill vibe as he lays it out sets me at ease, and I wonder if he's been preparing for this question for a while.

"You came out here first," he continues, "so I'll come see you next."

I glance at the elderly couple. The way they lean toward each other, nod, unconsciously touch—they've clearly been together for years. They've likely celebrated their fiftieth wedding anniversary, a thing Howie and I—no matter what could ever happen—will never do. But even still, we are them, right? And they are us. And we are the only ones in this spot, at this time, on not-even-the-coast-of-Oregon, that feels at once secluded and expansive and all the things you've ever believed a truly good morning could be.

And then—just because ever since we'd arrived in Ashland, everyone kept saying "the duck pond, the duck pond, the duck pond"—we went from breakfast to the duck pond. And at this duck pond, which is truly magnificent and of all the Ashland Things is by far the Ashlandiest, as we watch ducks sniff other ducks' asses, we sit, Howie with his arm around me, and kiss a little longer than the night before until Howie receives a text from the Praetorian Guard, prairie-dogging from their brunch.

What're you guys up to? they ask with a kissing emoji.

"What should I say?" Howie asks me.

"Just say, 'Maybe' . . ."

Before heading to the airport, we go to the Shakespeare Festival bookstore, where Howie helps me pick out a T-shirt for the Bear and a rosemary candle for me.

The herb rosemary, the card attached says, *is associated with love, lust, and remembrance . . .*

~

After flying back to Los Angeles and bidding a fond farewell to the Praetorian Guard, Howie and I walk to dinner around the corner from his place in Santa Monica. We order a dozen oysters and some wine. Howie asks me if there's ever a time that the Bear is with her dad for more than a weekend.

"Yes," I tell him, "as a matter of fact she is with him for three weeks in August, a little less than two months from now."

"Great," he says, "maybe you come out then, stay with me, and you write your book; I'll write my show, and we get to see each other every night, you know?"

"That sounds fun," I say.

Howie smiles; I smile; the waitress, now back with our oysters, smiles and tells us which ones are Kumamoto and which are Fishers Island, and then she leaves. And we are finally alone. And I look at him across the table, at the boy who is now a man whom I have known and who has known me for so long, and I think to myself, *My god, Howie, it's always been you.*

I cannot remember a thing about this dinner after this moment—what was said, how the cavatelli was prepared, or whether I had a crisp white or a sparkling rosé. Only that my feelings were as crisp and sparkling as that very first day at the Brittany message desk.

Sometime later we are back in Howie's living room. I check in for my flight and download my boarding pass to my iPhone. Then I sit next to Howie on the sofa. He leans over to kiss me. And this time, the ever-so-slight pause before the soupçon of tongue that usually heralds the inception of massive making out delivers the goods. And as the years shuffle like a deck of cards, I free-fall through a greatest hits of moments: I see us at the Brittany; I see us walking in Washington Square Park; I see us performing his play; I see us both inside his massive Marshall's parka after my performance in *The Maids*; I see us at Elephant & Castle / David's Pot Belly / The Polo Lounge; I see us having lunches at the long-gone 17th Street Cafe, just up the street from where we'd just had dinner, bathed in the pinky gold of a particularly magical magic hour. I see us tangled up, making out at our rehearsals, in his dorm room, in my apartment, at the Sherry-Netherland, just as we are right here, right now, with the very same sense of FUCKING FINALLY.

FINALLY, we are here.

FINALLY, there are no barriers, no distance, no limitations.

FINALLY, FINALLY, FINALLY . . .

"It never was there," we sang. *"I think it was here."*

"I love you," he says.

"I love you too."

"Thank you," he says, "for taking a chance—I know what a big step it was and how much courage it took."

"You have no idea how much this means to you," I say, smiling.

"Actually, I do," he says, brushing my hair out of my face. "It means everything . . ."

∿

On the plane, dazed with *l'amour* and sleepless for my third straight night yet somehow wide awake, I fish the candle I'd bought out of my bag. I want to inhale its rosemary for love, lust, and remembrance, to stay present in all the feels aglow within my being, the ones I never thought I'd experience ever again. And I notice now that the candle has not just a list of ingredients but also a name: *My Old Flame*.

Well.

What do you know?

It takes a long time for life to happen all at once.

I think of how, on the surface, Howie and I had stories and feelings and karma and dharma together and alone. These were the tangible truths that anyone could see. Why were we unable to glean the totality of what our many years of lunches and visits and messages and emails were saying to each other, if not explicitly than implicitly? Beyond the obvious, what we didn't know but perhaps always intuited was that beneath the surface was an endless ocean of limitless love that existed and persisted through space and time and obstacles real and imagined, self-imposed and at times necessary. We had finally stopped the chatter, the distractions, the excuses, the walls of protection long enough to grasp that we had always been looking for each other, even when we told ourselves we were not, and that in finding each other again, when we did, we found a part of ourselves.

DENOUEMENT

From: Howard Morris <REDACTED>
Date: June 15, 2015, at 4:32 PM
To: Nancy Balbirer <REDACTED>
Subject: You Still into Me?

Cuz I'm in LOVE. I'm in. I'm down. I've given up the rights to my heart (domestic and foreign).

Just a mere week ago, I was a normal person muddling through. Now my mind is on fire from morning until night with Nancy, Nancy, Nancy. Everything has changed.

And I'm a busy man! I'm not sitting around all day not doing shit! I do shit. All day. And in a few weeks I'll be doing shit and FILMING SHIT. That's a whole lot of shit.

But it's different now because . . . you're with me. Always, even if I don't actually see you (but I will, I promise you, in just a few weeks)! You are permanently lodged in my brain. How did you get into the permanent rotation in my thoughts?! Here's how my thoughts go: something else . . . Nancy. Blah, blah, blah . . . Nancy. Oh, here's something new and different . . . Nancy . . . Oh, time for lunch . . . NANCY . . . so then Grace and Nancy . . . What did you just say? Nancy.

I. CAN'T. STOP. THINKING. ABOUT. YOU.

WHEN DID I BECOME A CHARACTER IN A JANE AUSTEN NOVEL?!

Oh my god, you've got a starring role in my thoughts. You're the high-priced Hollywood star who gets a percentage of the gross. It's so true you don't know what you're missing until you find it . . .

Speaking of finding: So last year this chick tracks me down from Match.com (which even she noticed I hadn't been on in YEARS, like several years, so she knew I wouldn't see her response to me). But somehow she got enough from my "profile," googled me, got my name, then found me on Facebook, and called our one mutual "friend," who told her I was a great guy. She made this gargantuan effort to find me, finally sending me this whole long message on Facebook, because she felt like I might be **The One**. And for a minute, I was incredibly flattered. I mean, I thought, WOW—I'm sort of hot stuff to have a woman, a total stranger, go to such lengths to find me and ask me out! And then she tells me, after a couple of DMs back and forth, to feel free to google her. So I google. And I find out she's a writer. OK, that's cool, right? But then I see what she actually wrote . . . AND YOU CAN'T MAKE THIS UP—she wrote a best-selling book called ***Marry Him: The Case for Settling for Mr. Good Enough***.

Yes.

I COULDN'T EVEN WRITE HER BACK! I was totally HUMILIATED! What was I supposed to say? *It's so flattering that you think I might be Mr. . . . GOOD ENOUGH?!* Not even Mr. GOOD BUT NOT GREAT or MR. FUCKING "GOODBAR," but MR. If I Had **ANY** Other Options You'd Be Toast but Since I Don't, I Guess You're . . . GOOD ENOUGH! Can't you just picture how it would be, every time, getting together with new friends, telling "Our Story"? People looking on in envy, gushing: "**Wow, she really settled. Good for her!**" Or: "**He's incredibly mediocre! I'm so happy for you!**"

I. LOVE. YOU (of that I'm sure). You know I'm actually good. Period. Maybe even exclamation point! But I don't want to push it.

And I want you to know that I'm not going to let 3,000 miles or 10 billion miles stand between me having you and you having me and us taking care of each other and actually—dare I say it?—having JOY in our lives. Don't we deserve a little of that after all this time? To have that person who GETS YOU. The person who makes you laugh, most importantly, AT YOURSELF.

I'm DONE. I want to be with you FOREVER. I'm not even scared of the marriage institution we're both so eager to trash—WITH YOU.

I even had an "I'm going to marry Elaine Robinson" moment last night with Becca, who said to me, essentially, "These plans seem a little half-baked, Ben," to which I responded, "No, sir, they're fully baked."

This happened when I told her I'd found the woman I'm going to be with for the rest of my life, and she said, "How does Nancy feel?"

And I said, "I think she likes me."

And Becca started laughing.

But . . . here's the crucial thing: she was far from surprised. WHY DID THIS TAKE ME THIRTYSOMETHING YEARS TO REALIZE? The truth is, Nancy, I realized it a long time ago. ALL OF IT. And that is the truth. This is not a thirty-two-year-later, Howie-come-lately, I'm-in-love-with-Nancy-Balbirer revelation. I just had to get some stuff done.

Frankly, I had to get GOOD ENOUGH . . . for YOU. I just want to be clear. I. LOVE. YOU. And I always have . . .

Love, H

From: Nancy Balbirer <REDACTED>
Date: June 15, 2015, at 8:50 PM
To: Howard Morris <REDACTED>
Subject: The Triumph of Hope over Experience

Dear Mr. Not Good but Fanfuckingtastic (excited to see this as a monogram!),

I landed in NYC this AM feeling more exhilarated and at the same time more grounded than I've maybe ever been, and among the many, many reasons I want to thank you for what was truly the weekend-to-end-all-weekends is that it answered several questions that had bedeviled me for some time, namely:

Is there still, after all these years, a "thing" with Howie? (YES.)

What would happen if we ever went on a real date? Etc. (YASSSSSSSSS.)

But there was another question upon which our Weekend of Wow inadvertently shed light, something I was only able to unpack over the course of a sleepless red-eye, that opened my eyes REAL WIDE, a revelation I feel I MUST share.

Remember when I told you about my friend Jess, the one who dumped her horrible hubby and immediately hooked up with her kids' much younger (as in 20 years younger) "manny"?

Now, I'll admit that I tend to scoff at May-December relationships, but Jess's situation quite frankly gladdened me. YES, because I found it refreshing that the woman was the more, shall we say, *mature* of the couple, but mainly I was just really pleased for Jess: here was a woman who'd spent years—and I mean YEARS—in a fractious, miserable marriage that had taken forever to die, and once it did, she pulled her ass out of the dumpster and into the husky embrace of a sensitive stud, packed up the two kids, and moved from a ho-hum East Village two-bedroom with an eat-in kitchen to a rambling Classic Seven in Harlem with a formal dining room and three working fireplaces.

In short order she adopted two kittens; replaced her gray, grown-out shag with a chic, highlighted bob, and just like that, her deep-creviced perma-scowl was gone, and in its place a wide Julia Roberts grin.

Jess's kids began to thrive like never before with their happy mom, new abode, cute kitties, AND manly-manny-now-mom's-BF, who, wouldn't you know, within a month, moved in to join the party. And just when you thought things couldn't get any happier, they got not only *happier* but *healthier*: on his very first day living *en famille*, Jess bought the manny/BF a $1500 commercial-grade Vitamix, and from then on it was smoothies every morning for everyone!

OK—why am I telling you this? Well, because one Saturday, I was dropping the Bear off for a playdate, and just as we arrived, the manny/BF was whipping up one of his special Vitamixed concoctions.

"You have to try this," Jess said, handing me a plastic juice cup filled to the brim. "It looks awful, but it's got hemp hearts and bee pollen—I drink it every morning and it makes my skin absolutely *glow* . . ."

Now, look, it's entirely possible that what tasted to me like liquid bananas and sand was good for Jess's skin, but it was clear to anyone with eyes that what was making Jess glow wasn't the "hemp's heart," *it was her own.* Jess was in love, and that love was, at long last, being reciprocated.

It was an incredible thing to behold, Jess and the manny/BF, two seemingly disparate but perhaps kindred souls finding each other in the morass. But, like I was telling you in Ashland, as happy as I was to see Jess so fucking happy, a wave of sadness crept over me as I sipped my smoothie and the words *How the hell does Jess have a boyfriend?* scrolled across the marquee in my mind.

Now, to be clear, because I don't think I was, nor do I think I even fully understood this myself when we were discussing it before: this wasn't a covetous *How the hell does* Jess *have a boyfriend AND* I *DON'T*—I'd no sooner begrudge someone getting the things they deserve than I'd spend $1500 on a souped-up blender!

No.

This was HOW *the hell does Jess have a* boyfriend?

HOW the hell does Jess have a *boyfriend* when she could have just as easily been an embittered divorcée with zero interest in getting involved or hooking up, or whether she's still "got it," whatever "it" is or was that women are all supposed to be in possession of until the end of time lest they be relegated to the remainders' bin or worse?

How the hell does thoughtful, intelligent, successful Jess, after the soul-suck of terribleness that defines a failed relationship, say to herself, *Yes, absolutely, I am totally willing to give this a whirl again*?

And without missing a beat!

I mean, I love sushi, but after one bout of food poisoning it took **several years** for me to **even watch** *Seven Samurai* again, let alone eat raw tuna!

How, I asked myself, *did she do it?*

Was Jess a cockeyed optimist or an ill-advised *schmendrick*??

What about the ones who seem perfectly willing to traipse down the aisle as many times as it takes—Liz Taylor, for instance, who not only got married eight times but married AND DIVORCED Richard Burton TWICE? Or Zsa Zsa Gabor—she was married nine fucking times! You'd think after husband six or seven she'd say to herself:

You know some-sing, dahlink, I really suck at dis!

What sort of sanguine buoyancy must course through the veins of people like Jess or these serial matrimonists that makes them so able to believe that this time it'll stick? How the hell does Jess not think, as I did, that it was quite possible that this part of her life was over and that quite frankly maybe it was for the best because love and the attendant *mishegoss* had resulted in even worse *mishegoss*?

I didn't know.

But what I *also* didn't know, as I stood in Jess's fabulous Harlem kitchen, was why—if I was "fine" being alone, and not just "fine," mind you, but *beyond* fine; I felt freer and more myself than I ever had—was I so completely rattled? What was it about sipping Jess's BF's smoothie that had made me so utterly disconsolate when I was, at the same time, so genuinely delighted for my friend's boon?

It all got tucked, as so many things do, into the "Arcana, unsolved" file. And then . . .

A couple of weeks later, I flew from New York to Los Angeles and then on to Ashland, Oregon, to have a first date with a man I'd been in love with for 32 years, accompanied by 5 television writers, a producer, a publicist, an animator, and an actor. And suddenly, the feelings, the smoothie—it all started to make sense. Because as happy as I was and as at peace as I finally felt, it became abundantly clear that, just like the Barry Manilow lyric you quoted, "It's all very nice, but not very good."

It's like—you live in this sheltered, delicate little world, and you believe (or you tell yourself) that you're living. And then, somewhat miraculously, you get over yourself for five minutes and take a trip to the gloriously beautiful middle of nowhere and discover that while you are most certainly *alive*, you haven't actually been *living*.

And you further realize that there has been something so innocuous about it that it has almost, up till this very moment, been so subtle, so imperceptible, you could, if you wanted to, live (and die) like this without ever really knowing it.

I live in this wonderful, wacky, undeniably eccentric old building in New York City. And this wonderful, wacky, undeniably eccentric old building in New York City is, if you can believe it, supposedly afflicted with a "curse." And this "curse" seems to hamper only the love lives of its straight female residents (*"Whatevs—we live in a patriarchal society!"—the Curse*). I didn't find out about this "curse" until I was separated, but as soon as I did—I gotta be honest—I said to myself, *You know something, I'm not mad at it.*

Why? *Because it gave me an easy out.* Whether I believed in it or not, somewhere in the recesses of my psyche, I had, as my twisted little ace in the hole, the perfect excuse for not even fucking bothering (along with my myriad other excuses and so-called protections employed with a by-any-means-necessary fervor).

Anyway, in our building, aside from the de rigueur shrinks, dentists, acupuncturists (and even a doula) with offices on the first floor, we have, I kid you not, **a shaman**. Her office is right next to the mailboxes, and she's this very nice, modest, mild-mannered lady who just so happens to perform "soul retrievals." So, one day, not long after I'd first become aware of our building's malediction, I asked her if it were possible to catch a curse simply by living in a jinxed building. Like, do you automatically become *accursed* just by existing on blighted premises?

She goes, "Only if your energetic immune system happens to be low."

Oh.

So I asked her, assuming one's energy **is** a tad dimmed down (cough), if there was any way to break a curse or, more to the point, **break free of it**, and she says, "Yes, of course," and I ask how and she tells me a little about her practice, which sounded cool but expensive (after all, she's a shaman, not a wizard; she still has to pay the same overpriced rent we all do in an ever-gentrifying Chelsea!). But then she suggested some other, let's say, more down-market fixes, using stuff you might find in your pantry, like salt and lemon.

"Anything," she told me, "that gets you out of the trap of accepting a foregone conclusion to your story."

What the shaman was saying was so true. Curses, narrow belief systems, and fixed mindsets—they're about forgone conclusions, endings.

And THIS is how the hell Jess has a boyfriend. Jess, a woman who, like me, is dangerously close to being on AARP's mailing list, could have easily been turned off from relationships after being for so long in a bad one. But Jess, **unlike me**, understood that maybe the choice wasn't between a BAD relationship and NO relationship—maybe the choice was actually between a BAD relationship and a POTENTIALLY GREAT relationship.

"Your task," says the great Sufi mystic Rumi, "is not to seek for love, but merely to seek and find all the barriers within yourself that you have built against it."

Who knows if it'll work out with Jess and the manny—the point is, Jess is NOT DONE. Jess isn't accepting a "foregone conclusion" to her story because, on some level, she gets that her time here on this mortal plane isn't about "the end"; it's about writing and then rewriting the beginning over and over. It's about remaining open to the possibility of surprise.

And speaking of surprises:

On the flight home, aside from unpacking the profundities of Guru Jess, I was reminded of how when the thrice-divorced Erica Jong married the thrice-divorced Ken Burrows, the bride and groom sent out a wedding announcement that said: "Erica Jong and Ken Burrows are ASTONISHED to announce their marriage." Quoting Oscar Wilde, they referred to their fourth trip to the altar as "the Triumph of Hope over Experience." (Hope made them marry; experience made them sign a prenup—they "hoped" their love would last, but given their mutual histories, they couldn't know for sure. On their 10th wedding anniversary they threw their prenup in the wok and set it on fire—this one, they said, is for keeps . . .).

Like Erica and Ken, I, too, am ASTONISHED. I'm astonished that in the middle of 2015, in the middle of June, in the middle of Oregon, in the middle of life, I have found my forever person, in the form of a person I have known for most of my life, and yet as deeply astonishing as that is, it is even more astonishing that nothing has ever made more sense.

By the way, I know that we're every Barry Manilow song ever written, but do you know *which* Barry song you were actually quoting with "it's all very nice, but not very good"?

"Ready to Take a Chance Again."

And I am.

I love you, Howie, just like *Cats*—now and forever . . .

XOXOXO

N

What I couldn't know or imagine was that four Fridays later, when Howie flew to New York for our second date, after making love for the very first time in a hotel sixty-some-odd blocks to the south of the Sherry-Netherland, Howie will announce during a walk on the High Line in full view of London Terrace, "I think we need to get married." I said yes, of course, despite the fact that I could not know or imagine how or if we'd ever be able to live together in the same city. What I couldn't then know or imagine is that in a few months, when I tell my ex-husband, the Bear's dad, that Howie and I are together, his response will be "Oh—I love Howie!" Nor can I know or imagine that he will not only allow me the following year to take the Bear and move to Los Angeles, he will soon move there as well. I also can't know or imagine that in just a few months, the day after I turn fifty, my kid, Howie's biggest fan, will slip her hand into his as we walk together in Washington Square Park just as I had done thirty-two years before.

I also can't know or imagine as I sit basking in this kaleidoscope of love that this will be my last year in London Terrace Gardens. That in a year I will be saying goodbye to it and to Nat and Troy and Jenna and Bibi and Dorie and Susie and Rosalie and Paulie the Pothead, who oddly is the only one who tears up at this news. That in a year I will take one last look at the leaves, just starting to burst to life across the courtyard from the four rooms and foyer in which I had spent thirteen years. From when I was in my thirties and pregnant to in my fifties and starting menopause; where I'd lived when I had a baby and published a book and sold a second and buried a fur baby and would soon bury a second, our beloved Fosse. Where I'd lived as a married woman and a divorced woman and a remarried woman. I can't know or imagine that in exactly one year I will be staring at the leaves, saying to myself, *I will never know this place again as vividly*; that I'd never love something as much that wasn't really mine, that never *was* really mine, though it is as much a part of me as my heart. It's just something I have borrowed, and in a few weeks—after they dismantle and pull out our IKEA BILLY bookshelves that line the foyer, after they chop out the pine plank that is the makeshift desk in my "office" closet—it will belong to someone else.

One thousand five hundred and sixty-two Fridays after performing *Almost Romance*, forty-one Fridays after I flew out for our three-day date, and fifteen Fridays after he put a ring on it, Howie and I are married at City Hall in New York, where it all began. This particular Friday also happens to be Good Friday (bad day for Jesus, great day for us), which makes it not just a "Good" Friday, but the Best Friday Ever.

The Bear is my maid of honor; Howie's son, Dustin, is his best man; Candace Kahn is our witness; and one of my oldest friends comes to take pictures.

On the inside of Howie's wedding band, at the suggestion of the Bear, the inscription reads:

~~Almost~~ Romance N+H, March 25, 2016

"The *Almost* is gone, Mom, see?" the Bear says when she draws me her idea. "And you get to keep the *Romance* . . ."

After the ceremony at the Marriage Bureau, we repair to the Odeon in Tribeca with a few of our most treasured friends. Along with pink champagne and oysters, there are burgers and fries and the requisite extra-extra ketchup on the side, followed by sundaes with extra-extra hot fudge on the side—sauce-y people gonna sauce.

Over cocktails, our witness/matchmaker Candace asks to say a few words.

"People usually get together DESPITE me," she tells us.

We hear tales of her failed setups, her forced meddling ban at the behest of her husband, and of her penchant for writing the names of people she believed belonged together on napkins she'd date and put in a drawer.

She shares with us that after years of being filled to the brim with proof of her matchmaking shortfall, she tossed all the napkins and turned the drawer into a sanctuary for her staplers.

And though she "never wrote on a napkin again," Candace Kahn, successful television producer, never truly gave up on her potential to produce a successful match.

"Which is why," she adds conspiratorially, "when Howard had Bobby read Nancy's email aloud to the writers' room, I saw the chance I'd waited a lifetime for. The next day, at lunch at Hugo's in LA, I told my husband what was going on. He reminded me of my checkered history and the drawer-of-shame and made me promise to stay out of it. Then I went right home and friended Nancy on Facebook. Anyway, you all know the rest. I am so very happy for you. If I never do anything else in my life—this is a good thing. But really, it wasn't me. It was two hearts that had been waiting for each other. You had already written the story—we were just there to assure you that it was a good one. I am so honored to be part of this day and wish you every possible happiness. You all deserve it.

"Before we toast to the newlyweds, two things: First, this is from my Saturday babysitter, Wendy." *(Candace plays video on her phone of Wendy and Wendy's four kids shouting, 'Congratulations, Howard and Nancy!')* "And second, I lied. I *did* write on just one more napkin, and I've been saving it for you.

"And this one," Candace says, handing me the napkin, "like the love you share today, is yours to keep."

When single people hear the story of how Howie and I got together, they almost always get a wistful look in their eyes and invariably say some version of: "I wonder who from *my* past might be *my* person?"

"Live the question," I always tell them, "so that one day you will, without even noticing it, find yourself experiencing the answer." And then I tell them they should start scrolling through their Facebook friends because, hey—you never know.

I tell them that before my Year of Yes, I lived in an Epoch of Nope, not believing in, well, much, except for old movies (and Barbra). Now I'm one of those rabid born-agains, seeing the face of god everywhere, endowing the seemingly random with divinity.

I believe you should never blow off a good story just because it's challenging.

I believe that falling off the path *is* the path.

I believe that two things can be true.

I believe in Love after Love.

I believe in Barbra and Barry and that maybe the best *is* for last.

I believe in saving your napkins.

I believe you have no idea how much this means to you.

I believe if you count all your Fridays, one of the good ones will turn out to be the best Friday ever. Because even if you can't imagine it, cuz it's never happened, when it happens and it's finally here, you'll know because you'd imagined it all the time.

And anyway—what do you have to lose?

The
Beginning

ACKNOWLEDGMENTS

There are no words I can properly (or even improperly) assemble here to adequately thank my editor, Carmen Johnson, for her unerring eye, steadfast support, and endless patience. Carmen, I love working with you so much and can't wait for our next Monkey Bar hang. Christina Henry de Tessan, who asked all the right questions, then helped me take this whole thing apart and put it back together—thank you for your unfailing wisdom and for cheering me on.

Deep bows of gratitude to Emily Freidenrich and Emma Reh and the entire Little A Femipire who seriously kill it on the daily.

Erin Hosier is not just a great agent, she's an insanely cool chick whose savvy, kindness, and faith in me means the world. I am endlessly grateful to
Florence Falk,
George Sheanshang,
Alyssa Yoffie,
Annie Zaruba-Walker,

Elisa Casas for being with us that day at City Hall to snap the most beautiful wedding photos ever,

Kirsten Leigh Pratt, Avi Brosh, and the staff at Palihouse Santa Monica for graciously housing me so I could finish the first draft,

Cindy Miller for her love and friendship, and

Marc Alexander and Millicent Martin, whom I love beyond measure.

An author needs early readers, and I was lucky to have some of the best:
    Mike Albo,
    Michelle Grant,
    Josann McGibbon;
    and Suzanne Bukinik: thank you, thank you, thank you!

And finally, to my "characters"—the Praetorian Guard as well as the additional members of the *Grace and Frankie* writers' room:
    It takes a village of very funny people to help two writers not give up on a story just because it's challenging—thank fucking goodness for all of you.

Boo Boo Bear—it is the joy of my life that I belong to you. You are my baby, my best friend, and my witness, and I love you with all that I am.

And last but not least, to Nat and Troy and the rest of my friends at London Terrace Gardens (you know who you are): while we are no longer neighbors, you will *always* live right down the hall in my heart. I will never not miss you and will love you forever.

ABOUT THE AUTHOR

Nancy Balbirer is a writer and performer of stage and screen. She is the author of *A Marriage in Dog Years* and *Take Your Shirt Off and Cry*. She lives and loves in Los Angeles with her family.